The Morbidity of Culture

Stephanie Siewert / Antonia Mehnert
(eds.)

The Morbidity of Culture

Melancholy, Trauma, Illness and Dying
in Literature and Film

PETER LANG
Frankfurt am Main · Berlin · Bern · Bruxelles · New York · Oxford · Wien

Bibliographic Information published by the Deutsche Nationalbibliothek
The Deutsche Nationalbibliothek lists this publication in the Deutsche Nationalbibliografie; detailed bibliographic data is available in the internet at http://dnb.d-nb.de.

Cover Design:
© Olaf Gloeckler, Atelier Platen, Friedberg

Cover illustration:
Ryan Mosley
Art's House (painting will eat itself), 2011
Oil on Canvas, 215 x 186 cm
Courtesy Alison Jacques Gallery
and Galerie EIGEN + ART Leipzig/Berlin

ISBN 978-3-631-63614-5
© Peter Lang GmbH
Internationaler Verlag der Wissenschaften
Frankfurt am Main 2012
All rights reserved.

All parts of this publication are protected by copyright. Any utilisation outside the strict limits of the copyright law, without the permission of the publisher, is forbidden and liable to prosecution. This applies in particular to reproductions, translations, microfilming, and storage and processing in electronic retrieval systems.

www.peterlang.de

Contents

STEPHANIE SIEWERT
Reflections on the Culture(s) of Morbidity or the Morbidity of Culture 7

Transnational Melancholy

RÜDIGER KUNOW
"People between two countries always feel sorrow":
Some Preliminary Reflections on Transnational Affects 25

ANTONIA MEHNERT
"Ou libéré?"
Transnational Trauma in *Breath, Eyes, Memory* by Edwidge Danticat 37

Narratives of Illness—Illness Narratives

JOHN CARLOS ROWE
Disease, Culture, and Transnationalism in the Americas 55

MARC PRIEWE
Making Sense of Morbidity in Early American Autobiography 69

ARIANE SCHRÖDER
'Descent into Hell': The Cultural and Biomedical
Signification of Depression in William Styron's *Darkness Visible* 83

Aesthetics of Death

SANDRA POPPE
The Aesthetics of Death and Mourning in American Literature and Film 105

FREDERIKE OFFIZIER
Death of the Other: Dying, Alterity, and Appropriation 119

STEPHANIE SIEWERT
"As for France, the Nation has Disposed of You":
The Penal Colony as Morbid Space and Discourse of Life 139

Notes on Contributors 161

STEPHANIE SIEWERT

Reflections on the Culture(s) of Morbidity and/or the Morbidity of Culture

In his most recent film *Melancholia* (2011), Danish film director Lars von Trier stages the nemesis of our world as a panoramatic life-in-death experience: a deathly scenario envisioned as a moment of orgiastic sexual encounter.[1] A blue meteorite devours mother earth to the music of Richard Wagner's *Tristan and Isolde* (1859) and intones the last moments as an ecstatic neo-romantic *Liebestod*. The extinction of man could hardly be any more vital, or beautiful. Von Trier's film not only externalizes the pathologies of Western culture but is deeply invested in the history and (cultural) image repertoire of hysteria and melancholy.[2] *Melancholia* exemplifies in how far art *uses and abuses* a vocabulary and imagery of melancholy and is furthermore involved in its discursive production. Particularly interesting with regard to the topic of this essay collection on the "culture(s) of morbidity", the film illuminates the pathognostic function of art, which similarly calls attention to the "close alliance" of morbidity and productivity. Before I will display in more detail the value of this intricate connection for a discussion of culture and cultural representations, it is indispensable to explore the semantic field in which the dialectics of this relationship unfold.

The morbid is here understood to be an *expression of transience*, which not only spotlights the decay of life but moreover authors and authorizes the drive of renewal and the celebration of the instantaneousness of being in the face of death.[3] Nietzsche cherished the value of transience and argued that subjectivity is an act of self-creation which experiences its productivity in its transience. If everything flows, permanence and imperishability are "fictions", which *nolens volens* establish transience as a quality of truth. Equally Sigmund Freud conceives the frailness of beauty as an increase in value and bestows up-

---

[1] The scene epitomizes Heidegger's dictum that death lurks from the moment we come into being (279-311).
[2] The terms melancholia and depression are in my understanding not interchangeable, but have been used synonymously, especially since the twentieth century and with the development of psychoanalysis. In this paper I rely on both terms since Lars von Trier himself does not draw a clear line between melancholia and depression. The semantics and symbolism of melancholia and depression then often overlap see i.e. dark moods, lethargy, blackness, images of incorporation, planet Saturn, images of regression into the inner life.
[3] Within the ontological and the phenomenological approach of the *Daseins*-analysis decay is inherent to being-in-the-world, it constitutes the continual movement of the *Dasein* (Heidegger 279-311).

on the object a certain preciousness and uniqueness—an argument he elaborates on in his little-known essay "On Transience":

> Transience value is scarcity value in time. Limitation in the possibility of an enjoyment raises the value of the enjoyment. It was incomprehensible, I declared, that the thought of the transience of beauty should interfere with our joy in it. As regards the beauty of nature, each time it is destroyed by winter it comes again next year, so that in relation to the length of our lives it can in fact be regarded as eternal. The beauty of the human form and face vanish forever in the course of our own lives, but their evanescence only lends them a fresh charm. A flower that blossoms only for a single night does not seem to us on that account less lovely. Nor can I understand any better why the beauty and perfection of a work of art or of an intellectual achievement should lose its worth because of its temporal limitation. A time may indeed come when the pictures and statues which we admire today will crumble to dust, or a race of men may follow us who no longer understand the works of our poets and thinkers, or a geological epoch may even arrive when all animate life upon the earth ceases; but since the value of all this beauty and perfection *is determined only by its significance for our own emotional lives, it has no need to survive us and is therefore independent of absolute duration.* (my emphasis, Freud 305)

Within this approach of "relationality" the morbid is not a fixed category; it has no end or determination in itself, but has to be seen as a *significance* ascribed to the liminal state between the two normative markers of life and death. It is only perceivable in a temporal interval of past, present and future and is thus an immanent feature of worldly time. What Freud stresses at the end of the paragraph is furthermore the *signification* we give to the unavoidable presence of death in our lives, which refers to nothing less than the aesthetic. The morbid then delineates an aesthetic expression that attaches meaning to the physical, but also mental (and moral) decay.

Morbid themes served as warnings of the human hubris in ancient Rome and expressed a critique on worldly immersions in the *Vulgate* of the Middle Ages. *Memento mori* motifs or the personification of death in the *danse macabre* represented the universality of death and the vanity of earthly glories, just as *vanitas* symbols like the skull, rotten fruit, or hourglasses reminded man of the brevity of life. Later on in the seventeenth century, the baroque still lives and genre paintings displayed an interesting paradox in the representations of decay and mortality. The *morbidezza* (fleshliness) of the objects presented emphasized their sensuality and subtly reinforced the power of life. The sensual depictions and sometimes almost lusty exuberance, contradicted the didactic approach of installing a sense of humility in the beholder. The attempt of painters to capture the rottenness or decomposition of an object here point to a paradox encapsulated in the morbid expressions: in passing lies a certain accumulation of life. The morbid not only signifies what *is* life but first and foremost indicates the *presence* of the living, although *intentionally* the morbid prefigures death. Accordingly, it is a poetic principle that enfolds an analogous liminal space between the speech of life and the silence of death, between presence and absence, and exposes the paradoxical nature of art to be the reservoir of life and witness to its extinction.

The morbid then not only marks a state of decay but is simultaneously a sign of life and a catalyst of cultural processes. Morbid images—the figures and motifs of morbidity in literature and the visual arts—revitalize culture, as Margot Northey argues for nineteenth and twentieth century Gothic fiction: "[M]orbid expression probes beneath the surface of life, and helps to engender a fresh frame of meaning. Perhaps its strange and disturbing configurations of experience contribute to the reordering of our perceptions which, many would argue, is at the base of cultural revitalization" (110). Furthermore Northey observes:

> The very energy of much gothic and grotesque fiction supports a connection with cultural vitality as much as with cultural mortality. This being the case, those works which appear so death-ridden and frequently disintegrative may indeed be considered catalysts of regeneration. With good reason we may suppose that in culture, as in the natural world, death and decay are compost for new growth. (110)

What here refers to Gothic fiction could be expanded to fictional and autobiographical narratives of melancholy, trauma, illness and dying. As *moments of crystallizations* they engage with questions of "cultural vitality" and "cultural mortality", which also includes ethical questions of how to pursue a good life and how to deal with an often painful past and threatening present/future. As borderline situations, in which time is displayed in its existential drama, they equally bundle up suppressed desires and emotions produced by the frictions of what Habermas called "lifeworld" (common understandings, values) and "system" (the media of rationalization such as money and power) (1984: 87). The "pathologies" discussed here constitute points of departure to grasp the morbid as an attribute or quality ascribed to living organisms (animals, plants or persons), but also to objects, ideas, and concepts such as cultures and feelings.[4] Along these lines the morbid themes taken up in this collection are divided into three sections: 1. Transnational Melancholy, 2. Narratives of Illness—Illness Narratives, and 3. Aesthetics of Death. The articles explore individual and collective significations of social pathologies and collective dispositions, but also

---

4   Morbid, [ad. L. Morbid-us, f. Morb-us disease, f. Root of morī to die. Cf. F. Morbide, It., Pg. Morbido, Sp. Mórbido] 1. Of the nature of or indicative of disease; also, productive of disease, morbific, b. Of persons or animals, their parts, etc.: Affected by disease, diseases, unhealthy, c. Morbid anatomy: the anatomy of diseased organs or structures; 2. Of mental conditions, ideas, etc.: Unwholesome, sickly: chiefly applied to unreasonable feelings of gloom, apprehension, or suspicion. Hence of persons: Addicted to morbid feelings or fancies, 3. Painting. Of flesh-tints: Painted with morbidezza (referring to the life-like quality of flesh-tints); Morbidity: 1. the quality or condition of being morbid; a morbid state or symptom; pl. Morbid characteristics or ideas, 2. Med. Prevalence of disease; the extent or degree of prevalence in a district=Morbility (*The Oxford English Dictionary* 657, col. 1).

strategies of Othering concerning cultures, ideas or persons, and possibilities of self-empowerment *vis-à-vis* violent, conflicting and deathly encounters. The collection wants to give an impulse for cultural studies to consider the morbid as a productive category that could be further explored as an affix adhered to certain groups of people, cultures, or feelings in order to gain further insights from the ways foreignness is imagined. Besides being an attribute of distinction, the philosophical definition of the morbid as *the presence of death in life* calls up an array of *discourses of vitality and conviviality* in literature and the visual arts which need further examination.

For the purpose of clarity and in order to further elaborate these thoughts, I want to turn to the beginning of this introduction and provide, however abridged, a short analysis of the film *Melancholia* on the grounds of some of the aspects introduced so far. I argue that the film diagnoses and epitomizes the conditions of melancholy and furthermore generates conceptions of life and conviviality through its imagery of morbidity. More precisely, *Melancholia* employs a certain "morbid language" in order to expose, understand and communicate modern dispositions of melancholy and concomitantly positions the work of art and the artist within a tradition of modern "morbid eccentricity".

The film magnifies the internal conflicts of a group of people at a wedding party and the time after when the main protagonist, Justine, falls deeper into depression and is taken care of by her sister Claire in a castle in the countryside. While the first part of the film is focusing on Justine's condition, the second part stays close to Claire's anxiety and narrates the arrival of the blue/black planet which moves at 60.000 miles an hour towards earth. The film focuses on the development of beautiful Justine, who is caught up in the internal conflict of conformity and desire. At her wedding party she realizes that she had never wanted to marry Michael, a nice, uncomplicated and attractive young man and that an indefinable and noncommunicable fear leaves her paralyzed amidst her dancing and celebrating guests. The community at display, Justine's family and friends, serves as a microcosm to expose the dysfunctionality of modern societies—their decadent and narcissistic character. Justine's father is a hedonistic man, who leaves the scene at a moment when Justine needs his advice and her cynical mother despises the marriage (one might say any human relationship) as an illusion and false hope and tells Justine "to wake up". Both parents have nothing to give in terms of emotional support.

Although it might be tempting to speculate about a story of betrayal, of loss and bitter disappointment, von Trier allows only a brief glimpse into the abyss of their relationship and denies simple explanations for Justine's illness. Rather, the revulsion Justine feels for this world, the individual crisis, serves as a mirror for the *social pathology of the time*, and equally fuels the idea of melancholia as an *anthropological constant* precisely through allusions to literature, popular discourses and the visual arts, and is thus reviving an antagonistic perception of melancholy most prominently presented in Shakespeare's *Hamlet*

(1603) and Robert Burton's *The Anatomy of Melancholy* (1621). The film takes up early modern conceptions of melancholy as Justine is drawn to the black planet resembling Saturn, which was believed to affect the intellectual's mind, and held responsible for melancholic moods in the fifteenth century. Correspondingly, Justine is portrayed as brilliant and thoughtful, moreover she seems to possess almost psychic powers since during a conversation with her sister she admits that she "knows things".[5] Her ability to feel more profoundly than anyone else underlines an assumption that can be traced back to Pseudo-Aristotle and his famous statement that all great men are melancholics, a view that was revivified in the Neoplatonic tradition and Italian Humanism. Marsilio Ficino's book *Three Books on Life* (*De Vita Libri Tres,* 1480-1489) contained an influential passage on the causes and methods of treatment for melancholy and was likewise a narrative of his own condition. Accordingly, Julia Kristeva has emphasized in her study *Black Sun: Melancholy and Depression* (1989) that "[f]or those who are racked by melancholia, writing about it would have meaning only if writing sprang out of that very melancholia" (3). Here Lars von Trier positions himself within the tradition of works on melancholy which were diagnostic and therapeutically at the same time, and which ultimately served as narratives of self-empowerment.

Von Trier's *Melancholia* also seems to nurture a morbid eccentricity flaunted by authors of the *fin de siècle* like Charles Baudelaire or modernists of the early twentieth century, such as Thomas Mann. He shares their religious empathy for decay, the obsession with morbidity and death, the satiation with the "ordinary language" and the consequent connection of pathos and pathology. There is a moment when Justine lies naked on the rocks of the riverbank, illuminated by the light of the blue planet and awaiting the embracement of death, which calls into mind the last poem of Baudelaire's *Fleur du Mal* (1857), "Le Voyage", where the narrating voice imagines his own death and calls out to the captain, the allegorical death: "It's time, Old Captain, lift anchor, sink! / *The land rots; we shall sail into the night; / if now the sky and sea are black as ink* / our hearts, as you must know, are filled with light. […]— *heaven or hell, who cares?*" (my emphasis, Baudelaire 185).

Likewise, the film does not display fantasies of salvation, since Justine stresses that we are all alone and discards all chances of a new beginning somewhere else in the universe. Trier emphasizes the *in-betweeness* that generates images of transcendence. The apocalyptic end becomes a frame narrative to think and negotiate the way we behave facing the end of our lives.[6] Here the

---

5   At the wedding party the wedding planner invites the guests to estimate how many beans have been filled into a jar. No one could guess the exact number except for Justine.
6   See here the parallels to the black plague in Boccaccio's *Decameron* (1349-53), where ten young people flee from the plague in Florence and take shelter in a villa in the hills of Fiesole. The pestilence literally and metaphorically provides the frame narrative to

film provides a variety of possible reactions ranging from negation, anxiety, curiosity and relief. Claire, Justine's caring but always nervous sister, is scared and tries to circumvent the thought of death by desperately clinging to the scientific explanations of her husband. John refuses the idea that his life will end shortly and swears by his knowledge of astrology. He belittles his wife in her fears but kills himself in the moment he realizes that science has betrayed him. Justine, however, is thrilled and grows calmer the minute the planet moves towards earth. She does not fear the collision. She tells Claire that the "earth is evil" and that they have already reached the Inferno since life in company is what constitutes hell. Facing darkness she finds redemption from the finitude of life, the burden of surviving in this world has been taken from her since there will be no tomorrow. The moment of approaching death is a moment of recognition. Freed, she apparently "loses it" for everyone else, but finds herself in the shadow of the dark planet. In the darkest hour, where neither immortality nor the Inferno might frighten her, liberated from illusion, she discovers her *Eigentlichkeit* (authenticity) in the "freedom towards death" (Heidegger 311). For the first time her state of mind equals the external circumstances, not only her "existence is on the verge of collapsing" (Kristeva 3) but the whole world.

Yet, although Trier clearly draws on the morbid imagery of European romantic and decadent literature, he is not interested in the *tabula rasa* topos of modernism as the last line of Baudelaire's poem "Le Voyage" suggests: "Through the unknown, we'll find the new" (185). He is much more pessimistic about what might await us. In "The Ideology of Modernism", Marxist critic Georg Lukács has argued that for (some) modernist writers the morbid and the psychopathological was a "tertium ad quem," an intentional aesthetic strategy to voice a protest against the rationalizing and de-individualizing effects of modernity (150). The "new" was then still bearing the vision of a better world. Although "at each period—depending on the prevailing social and historical conditions—psychopathology was given a new emphasis, a different significance and artistic function" (Lukács 150), with the beginning of World War I morbidity became an "all-pervading obsession" (ibid). Lukács acknowledges that modernist artists' explorations of the morbid had been ambitious and vital "discussions," furthermore "[t]hese writers are not wholly wrong in believing that *psychopathology is their surest refuge; it is the ideological complement of their historical position*" (my emphasis, 151), but their "morbid eccentricity" had eventually been an "abstract gesture," an escapist ideology without clear definition and real engagement. Accordingly one might ask, if the morbid has even more so become "an empty gesture" in the twentieth and twenty-first centuries. Has it lost its vitalizing force and become a rhetoric too often voiced in (post)modernism to be understood and seen in the wake of "real" catastrophes?

---

indulge in a critical investigation of the Italian society of the 14th century. The deathly threat becomes a catalyst to think and narrate alternative ways of life.

Is the current boom of vampires, werewolves, Armageddon's and "last man standing" in literature and film an expression of *ennui*, a way to escape "the prosaic life under capitalism" (Lukács 150), or are they rather a moral protest against the profanation of life?[7] For many contemporary art works it seems more and more difficult to differentiate between the decorative and the ethical function of the morbid.

Concerning *Melancholia*, I would argue that Trier's morbid biomorphous imagery[8] restores the organic as an affirmation of life in a time of digital reproduction and thus recounts an enlightenment and romantic discourse of harmony and unity, of order in chaos, and homogeneity over plurality which had then been employed to formulate a critique on the consequences of modernity: artificiality, disintegration and individualization (Scherpe 10-11). However, one could also emphasize that his film inscribes itself into the modern pathological discourse of denial and can be analyzed as an example for an argument brought forth by Phillipe Ariès (1974) concerning the negation of death in modernity: We are then confronted with a group of decadent, beautiful young people who float through a setting somewhere in the countryside which consists of an old castle, a golf course, a great view of the ocean and a wild forest with a stream.

Like the figures in a play the protagonists are placed in the scene, moving dream-like from one site to another. As a beautiful interpretation of "La mort est un éternel sommeil", the death bed becomes a *locus amoenus*—with an essential twist: Justine and her family are not (yet) dead, but for all we see they already are their "beautiful corpses" (Adorno/Horkheimer 216). This conclusion confirms that the aesthetic representation of death displayed in the film legitimizes a last, orgiastic or suicidal excess, which, as Thomas Macho (2010) argues, could be seen as particular to modern Western cultures. In the last scene of the film, Justine, Claire and her son take a feigned refuge in a "magic cave," a tipi made up of sticks, while behind them the blue planet rises from the horizon and finally takes them away in a gigantic fireball. Their death is presented as an almost supernatural "event" that ultimately negates the negativity of death and exposes the film itself as a melancholic act.

---

7   With regard to the pathologization of the aesthetic discussed here, Johann W. von Goethe had detected in romantic art an obsession with figures such as the vampire and the *Doppelgänger*: "Im Altertum spuken dergleichen Erscheinungen nur vor wie seltene Krankheitsfälle; bei den Neuern sind sie endemisch und epidemisch geworden" (629). The critique displayed here has then to be analyzed in more detail within a "rethorics of a pathologization of the aesthetic," which cannot be further elaborated due to the limitations of an introductory note.

8   In the egg-shaped planet, the cell and the uterus refigure as the cosmos and cave of life, moreover the egg symbolizes the in-betweeness of growth and decay, of creation and entropy.

From my singular observations on the dialectical relationship of productivity and morbidity, which might, applied to other scenarios, offer valuable insights on the state of individual and collective pathologies, I would now like to venture a short excursus on the role of the morbid in cultural history. The subject of morbidity certainly calls for a historical and comparative perspective if one assumes that is always already constituted against a more vital state. Languages of crisis and anxiety mainly develop from the phantasmagorical image of a brighter, more "livable," or "innocent" past or future. Accordingly, a historical perspective can make us realize that current "rhetorics of decay" are neither singular, nor particular to our time and culture and that they often disguise the reasons of their emergence and an active search for solutions. Thus it becomes crucial to ask: What exactly we are looking for when we turn to the morbid?

One might propose that the morbid examined with regard to historical power relations is foremost an ascription of the "winner" in history. It then becomes a modifier of the colonized, the Other and hence a rhetoric strategy of hegemonial discourses, which have found a murderous climax in e.g. the racial theories of colonialism, theories of degeneration and in modern eugenics. Assuming that a morbid language and imagery marks a crisis and destabilization of the subject (as in the thought or experience of death), it has to be integrated somehow into a cyclical or causal narrative to be able to perceive it as meaningful. In the evolutionary and naturalist theories which developed from a theory of nature, culture was perceived analogously as an endless process of becoming and passing.

The morbid had served as an important category in the cultural morphologies from Hippocrates, Johann Wolfgang von Goethe, Wilhelm von Humboldt, to Oswald Spengler's *The Decline of the West* (1918) and Arnold J. Toynbee's *A Study of History* (1934-61). It was furthermore most vividly expressed in the theories of cultural hegemony in the racial anthropologies of the nineteenth century as in Joseph Arthur Comte de Gobineau's *An Essay on the Inequality of the Human Races* (1853-55). In the language and culture of late nineteenth century evolutionary naturalism the biological circle of birth and decay served as an explanatory model for the rise and fall of civilizations. This assumption then "punctuates a Western philosophy, politics and religion, from, say, Plato to Rousseau to Hegel" (Pick 18), following the argument that "[e]very civilization had a history: a beginning, an interlude of growth and a time of contraction and decline [...]" (Sinai qtd. in Pick 18). The "histories of civilizations" were then equally narratives of progress, which did not only imply an evaluation of cultures on the basis of their moribundity—taken as a sign for their level of civilization—, but moreover provided conclusions on the nature of their "spirit" and the value of their cultural production, such as literature, pottery, but most of all, architecture. These factors then built a complex system of valuation to underline 1. an often displayed nostalgia for the classic

(Greek) cultures and 2. the cultural hegemony of the West over e.g. African or Asian cultures.

Yet, while the morbid Other was sought outside Western culture, the entourage of Western progress—urbanization and secularization—had produced unruly desires and a certain moral degeneration within, a decline symptomatic to reason itself, as Rousseau had argued (Pick 19). One might assume that with the age of Enlightenment, but especially from the mid-nineteenth century onwards, the morbid became a much more mobile and political category and turned into a critique of the West, more precisely, a critique of modernity. Conspicuous consumption, excessive individuality, financial crashes and the World Wars were then analyzed as *both causes and signs of a culture of/in decay*.[9] Valorization and rejection of the morbid became two sides of the same coin. Moreover, as the language of menacing catastrophe and decay surfaced in most areas of public life, it was often accompanied by a diagnostic discourse. Art was here not an exception, as the medical approach provided the methodological parameters to analyze the perception and impact of art itself. In his study *Verlust der Mitte* (1948), and especially in the chapter *Analogia morbi*, the Austrian art historian Hans Sedlmayr voiced a critique of nineteenth and twentieth century modern art by analyzing modern styles as symbols and symptoms of an inner crisis of society. His methodology was based on a description of the symptoms and a "diagnosis" from which he ventured a prognosis concerning the social pathologies.

This almost virulent and prolonged "vocabulary of disease", which disseminated in the nineteenth century, is described by Richard Overy with regard to the twentieth century and the years between the World Wars:

> Physicists exploded the balanced Newtonian universe; biologists exposed the power of genetic inheritance and the possibility of degeneration; psychologists suggested that rational modern man was a chaos of instincts and urges within; chemists and engineers praised a new material environment, but also produced new weapons of terrible destructive powers; social science argued that the existing capitalist social system was corrupt and insupportable [...] The language used for much of this discourse was explicitly morbid, partly because a good deal of it was fueled by the human sciences, through which the vocabulary of disease, physical decline or mental instability could be applied metaphorically to the wider world of politics and social development. (4)

The medicalization of language suggested the possibility of cure, yet there was no uniform remedy for what had become an almost rhizomatic structure of crisis—a perception that up until now seems to prevail (Overy 4-5). Today, the

---

9 I would not so much speak of a revival, but in the last years diagnostic books on the decline of culture and the decay of Western societies have flooded the market almost like the diagnostic doom-literature at the end of the nineteenth and the first half of the twentieth century, of whom the most influential work was Freud's *Civilization and its Discontents* (1930).

ambiguity of science, spurred by biotechnology and biogenetics, fuel the morbid atmosphere and it seems that a certain *angst* has infused most areas of life from social interactions, to the economy or the environment. An all-consuming nervousness prevails, a continual jittering between the "best self" (Goffman) and the "exhausted self" (Ehrenberg). Accordingly, Alain Ehrenberg called depression the "illness of autonomy" and indeed one might ask, if the mobility of our world has not rather fostered a language and atmosphere of morbidity. Have the unbound possibilities for some, and the collision between the imagined lives and real economic possibilities for others, a more vitalizing or rather mortifying effect? Hence, what has been excluded so far and shall be further analyzed according to the atmosphere of uncertainty, are the specific anxieties produced by migration and diaspora, a certain transnational affectivity and sense of crisis which cannot be easily integrated in the general rhetorics of a "morbid modernity" and yet are part of the social pathologies of modernity (colonialism, imperialism, migration). Paul Gilroy and Anne Anling Cheng, among others, have argued that there are specific transnational affects, like melancholy or mourning, which equally yet differently, affect the "mainstream" societies and migrant communities and have to be considered in the discussions of multicultural societies.

With regard to these developments, the first section of this collection deals with anxieties and traumatic encounters as they are experienced by people whose biographies are dispersed across continents. Rüdiger Kunow will introduce the first part on transnational affects by taking up and extending more recent theories on the role of affects for diasporic communities. His article examines the dynamics of affective negotiations within the binary oppositions of "they" and "we," "inside" and "outside" and further stresses the importance of affects in the constitution of the individual body and the body politics in the theory and practice of mobility. He focuses on the specific affective ties of migrants from the Indian Subcontinent in America and explores the dissemination of affects such as melancholia, fear and dread produced by intergenerational conflicts in social and aesthetic expressions. His article moreover stresses the problematic dealings with the "presence" of the morbid in the smallest unit of society, the family, as elderly family members more and more represent the Other—a reality that is often ignored in the critique of mobility.

Antonia Mehnert similarly focuses on problematic intergenerational negotiations and the communication of transnational trauma in US-Caribbean writings. In her analysis of Edwidge Danticat's *Breath, Eyes, Memory* (1994) she explores what Kathleen Brogan calls the "pathologies of memory," which "take on a cultural and political significance, reflecting a society's inability to integrate with the present both traumatic experience and a pre-catastrophic lost past" (Brogan 7). Through the text these narratives aim to overcome the "explanatory mode" and demand an articulation/voicing of the pain produced by terror and violence in the wake of colonialism. Mehnert's article then also discusses the difficulty of gaining access to a lost or denied past and the revitalization of traumatic experiences within the "imaginary" resurrections.

The signification of social pathologies and illness constitutes a chief concern of the second section on bioculture and narratives of illness. Within a *globalization of disease*, the dialectical structure of representations of disease (Gilman 2-3) shall here move to the center of attention as much as the "real" effects of disease on the cultural, ecological and moral environment. Sandra Gilman emphasizes how the "anxiety of self-control" (3) has turned our fears outwards, projecting it onto others who seem particularly prone to sickness (2-3). Moreover disease representations can be said to be "both autobiographical, as expressions of an individual sense of pathogenic threat, and culturally specific, as they reflect the characteristic ways larger social groups see themselves and others" (Bewell 5). In the following articles the "cultural encounter" triggers the morbid as a marker of differentiation, but also of (spiritual) recognition and as a possibility for the empowerment of the "self" within a certain cultural hermeneutics of illness.

John Carlos Rowe investigates the cultural and environmental effects of communicable diseases during the conquest of the New World and the Euro-American encounters with Native Americans in the nineteenth century. His article challenges theories of cultural and biological "superiority" with regard to the spread of communicable diseases in the Americas and adds another important perspective to questions of intention for cultural and environmental impacts of diseases. Rowe furthermore stresses that the consequences of diseases for the socio-cultural, environmental, psychological and ethical systems of societies are yet to be further explored and aims for a critical reassessment of interdisciplinary perspectives on the impact of disease uniting cultural studies and biological science in order to come to a more thorough understanding of the "techniques" of imperialist control.

Marc Priewe's article further nuances an interdisciplinary junction which positions the morbid within a conflictual narrative of physical and moral decay. His investigations focus on the rising congruence of medical and religious discourses in Puritan New England and their competing authoritative claims in the interpretation and the healing of the body. For the Puritan communities, questions remained if the interference of man was reconcilable with God's divine plan in which illness was regarded as a token of misconduct that had to be chastised. Accordingly, Priewe discusses the connection between morbidity and morality in the symbolic encodings of illness in Puritan spiritual autobiographies in Colonial America. His analysis of writings by John Winthrop, Thomas Shepard, Anne Bradstreet, John Dane, and Increase Mather explores the different readings of illness as signs of sin, approaching apocalypse or as an explanation for certain incidents in communal life.

The subsequent article by Ariane Schröder ties in with Marc Priewe's conclusions by exploring in how far a certain "illness-masterplot" refigures in contemporary illness narratives, thus locating diseases like depression within a certain interpretative frame of illness that is based on a dominant biomedical discourse. This narrative is then adopted and challenged by individual experiences of those affected by illness: patients, doctors, family and friends. Her analysis of William Styron's *Darkness Visible: A Memoir of Madness* (1990) not only shows in how far readings of illness are necessarily relying on familiar cultural and religious images of illness in order to make sense of individual sufferings, but also stresses the responsibility of the humanities to provide a counter discourse to the biomedical authority.

The last section deals with representations of death and death-like figurations in modern literature and film. Popular contemporary discourses, with their "fitness-first" agenda and gloss-over aesthetics try to prevent at any cost what has the slightest taste of the morbid. "New is always better," seems to be the device of the time,[10] yet this motto only tells half the truth since contemporary Western and highly industrialized cultures move between the paradox of extending life at any cost, and a certain almost neo-romantic weariness with/of life that fosters the desire to end it with all force in an orgiastic "event" (Macho 2010). Accordingly, the current popularity of TV Shows and films such as *Dexter*, *Nip-Tuck*, *Six Feet Under*, *Vampire Diaries*, *True Blood*, or *Twilight* indicate on the one hand an obsession with morbidity and on the other hand a refusal to confront the finality of death. The morbid is here explored as an important category in the discussions of (post)modern biopolitics, foremost in terms of agency and representability, but also with respect to its role in the construction of precarious identities.

In her opening to the section on aesthetics of death, Sandra Poppe reflects on more recent developments in American literature, film and TV-productions, precisely Joan Didion's *The Year of Magical Thinking* (2005), Don DeLillo's short novel *The Body Artist* (2001), the HBO-series *Six feet under* (2001-2005) by Alan Ball and the film *The Fountain* (2006) by Darren Aronofsky. She concludes that the aesthetics of death in contemporary culture are much more complex and cannot easily be aligned with cultures of denial. The particular "language" of literature and film then not only offers different ways of how to deal with the inconceivability of death through e.g. identification and empathy but is foremost characterized by an aesthetic distance which creates a safe space of encounter with death.

Frederike Offizier's article challenges normative conceptions of death in Western societies and highlights the performative aspects of dying and the encounter with death as an experience of alterity and appropriation. Departing from the assumption that cultural representations expose a fictional nature of

---

10   The most trenchant perspective on the modern dilemma of immortality is probably Oscar Wilde's *The Picture of Dorian Gray* (1890/91) which dramatizes the appeal and burden of eternal youth.

the self and the Other, she illustrates that every negotiation with death is essentially refigured in the symbolic and understood within the sociality of dying. In addition, Offizier stresses that the performativity of dying restores the ineluctable elements of spectacle in both the Other and the self which equally affect the comprehension of the corporeality of dying—a discourse often denied and furthermore suppressed by (post)modern biomedical discourses.

Stephanie Siewert's article defines the morbid as an attribute of the deviant, which, in the case of the French penal colonies, was connected to the space of the penal island and a metropolitan discourse of civilization and savagery. The article focuses on representations and figurations of the morbid in Franz Kafka's *The Penal Colony* (1919) and Franklin J. Schaffner's *Papillon* (1973) and highlights the entanglements of imperial, racial and penal discourses in the nineteenth and twentieth century. Looking more closely at the precariousness of "dispensable" existences as displayed in the aesthetic representations, the article furthermore considers the ontological connections of decay (*Verfall*) and waste (*Abfall*) in nineteenth century theories of degeneration and deportation.

In conclusion, I want to take up the question in how far the morbid might be a critical category for cultural studies and cultural theory. Here, one might refer to the more general argument by Theodor W. Adorno that after Auschwitz all modern critique has become essentially morbid, moreover, as Foucault once argued, every theory has to be thought through Auschwitz, so as cultural critics we do not only speak *of and about* the morbid, but first of all *through* the morbid. Our relationship with the dead, our ability to mourn the dead, as Adorno and Horkheimer stress, then defines a (seemingly lost) consciousness for our history. In their note "On the Theory of Ghosts" from the *Dialectic of Enlightenment* (1944), they state that, "the conscious horror of destruction [...] creates the correct relationship with the dead", which also means the "correct" relationship to ourselves as historical beings and beings *in* history[11]. This reflects a certain responsibility for cultural studies to raise awareness of the ghosts we are living with, but it also means to turn a critical eye on our institutional and professional modalities of ghostliness.

As for the humanities the rhetorics of morbidity are employed with every change of paradigm, considering the times critics have proclaimed the death of the *grands récits*, the death of the author, the death of referentiality, the death of the text and the birth of new media. The constant calls for renewal are not only due to the inherent drive of science to explore new fields of research, or "unknown territories". The mortality rate of paradigms and turns can almost be called obsessive and at times absurd in its rigor and is often used as a strategy of professional ambition. One might as well argue that the humanities them-

---

11 The original German expression adds an ethical level to this relationship. Here the "correct relationship" is the "rechte Verhältnis", which attains to the German word "Recht" (right, law). Derrida takes up this denotation in his hauntology Spectres of Marx (1993).

selves have dwelled in the "spectral turn", "haunted" by an eighteenth/nineteenth centuries European vision of *Geisteswissenschaft* (*sciences humaine*) and "hunted" by the natural sciences (Neuroscience, biotechnology), always pressured to produce useful and serviceable knowledge. Furthermore, one might observe a heightened sense for the morbid, expressed not only in the rhetorics of self-enhancement in the humanities, but also as a specific *Geister-Wissenschaft*—which refers to the feeling that in an accelerated globalization more things are lost than found and continuously haunt our societies. At times, there are almost too many ghosts to deal with.

Finally, the morbid discourse encapsulates the more "real" menace of budget cuts and the death of language departments in Europe and the U.S. Do we, literally, wither away? Again, this is also a question of our moral choices and a society's decision of what it considers to be vital and productive—significant for our emotional lives. We hope to show in the articles presented in this collection that the *Geistes*wissenschaft is still a spirited dialogue partner.

Works Cited

Adorno, Theodor W., and Max Horkheimer. "Theory of Ghosts". *Dialectic of Enlightenment*. Repr. London: Verso, 2008. 215-216.

Ariès, Philippe. *Western Attitudes Toward Death: From the Middle Ages to the Present*. Trans. Patricia M. Ranum. Baltimore, MD: Johns Hopkins University Press, 1974.

Baudelaire, Charles. *The Flowers of Evil*. Eds. Marthiel & Jackson Matthews. Trans. Robert Lowell. NY: New Directions, 1963.

Bewell, Alan. *Romanticism and Colonial Disease*. Baltimore: Johns Hopkins Univ. Press, 1999.

Brogan, Kathleen. *Cultural Haunting. Ghosts and Ethnicity in Recent American Literature*. Charlottesville: Univ. of Virginia Press, 1998.

Burton, Robert. *The Anatomy of Melancholy*. Oxford : Clarendon Press, 1989.

Pick, Daniel. "Introduction". *Faces of Degeneration. A European Disorder, 1848-1918*. Cambridge: Cambridge Univ. Press, 1989.

Cheng, Anne Anling. *The Melancholy of Race: Psychoanalysis, Assimilation, and Hidden Grief*. New York: Oxford University Press, 2001.

Derrida, Jacques. *Specters of Marx. The State of the Debt, the Work of Mourning and the New International*. Trans. Peggy Kamuf. New York: Routledge, 1994 [1993].

Ehrenberg, Alain. *The Weariness of the Self: Diagnosing Depresssion in the Contemporary Age*. McGill-Queen's Press, 2009.

Ficino, Marsilio. *Three Books on Life*. Binghamton. New York: Center for Medieval & Early Renaissance Studies, 1989.

Freud, Sigmund. "On Transience". *The Standard Edition of the Complete Psychological Works of Sigmund Freud*. Vol.14. Ed. and Trans. James Strachey et al. London: Hogarth Press, 1973.

---. *Civilization and Its Discontents* (1930). The Standard Edition of the Complete Psychological Works of Sigmund Freud. Ed. and Trans. James Strachey et al. Vol. 21. London: Hogarth Press, 1961.

Gilman, Sander. *Disease and Representation. Images of Illness from Madness to AIDS*. 3rd print. Ithaca, Cornell University Press, 1994.

Gilroy, Paul. *Postcolonial Melancholia*. New York: Columbia Univ. Press, 2005.

Gobineau, Arthur de. *Essai sur l'inégalité des races humaines*. Paris: Firmin-Didot,1853-1855.

Goethe, Johann Wolfgang von. *Berliner Ausgabe. Kunsttheoretische Schriften und Übersetzungen*. Bd. 18. Berlin: Aufbau Verlag, 1960. 602-632.

Goffman, Erving. *The Presentation of Life in Everyday Life*. Repr. London: Penguin Press, 1971.

Habermas, Jürgen. *The Theory of Communicative Action*. Trans. Thomas McCarthy, Cambridge: Polity, 1984-87.

Heidegger, Martin. *Being and Time*. Translated by John Macquarrie and Edward Robinson. Oxford: Blackwell, 1962.

Kristeva, Julia. *Black Sun. Depression and Melancholia*. Trans. Leon S. Roudiez. New York: Columbia Univ. Press, 1989.

Lukács, Georg. "The Ideology of Modernism". Eds. Terry Eagleton and Drew Milne. *Marxist Literary Theory: a Reader*. Oxford: Blackwell, 1996. 141-162.

Macho, Thomas H. *Todesmetaphern: Zur Logik der Grenzerfahrung*. Frankfurt/M.: Suhrkamp, 1987.

---. *Vorbilder*. München: Fink, 2010.

Macho, Thomas, and Kristin Marek eds. *Die Neue Sichtbarkeit des Todes*. München: Fink, 2007.

Melancholia. Dir. Lars von Trier. Perf. Kirsten Dunst, Charlotte Gainsbourg, Alexander Skarsgård and Kiefer Sutherland. Zentropa Entertainments. 2011. Film.

Milton, John. *Milton's "L'Allegro" and "Il Penseroso"*. Repr. of the ed. publ. in London, 1860. London: Scolar Press, 1975.

Nietzsche, Friedrich. *Sämtliche Werke. Kritische Studienausgabe. Nachlass*. Bd. 15. Giorgio Colli and Mazzino Montinari. München/New York: Dt. Taschenbuch Verl., 1980.

Northey, Margot. *The Haunted Wilderness. The Gothic and Grotesque in Canadian Fiction*. Univ. of Toronto Press, 1976.

Overy, Richard. *The Morbid Age. Britain and the Crisis of Civilization, 1919-1939*. London: Penguin Books, 2009.
Scherpe, Klaus. "Faszination des Organischen. Eine Vorbemerkung". *Faszination des Organischen: Konjunkturen einer Kategorie der Moderne*. Eds. Hartmut Eggert, and E. Schütz and P. Sprengel. München: Iudicium-Verl., 1995. 7-11.
Shakespeare, William. *Hamlet*. Facs. repr. of the ed. publ. in London, 1600. Oxford: Clarendon Press, 1964.
Sedlmayr, Hans: *Verlust der Mitte. Die Bildende Kunst des 19. Und 20. Jahrhunderts als Symptom und Symbol der Zeit*. Wien/Salzburg: Otto Müller Verlag, 1948.
Spengler, Oswald. *The Decline of the West*. 2 Vols. Trans. Charles Francis Atkinson. New York: A. A. Knopf, 1926-28.
The Oxford English Dictionary. Vol. VI, L-M. Oxford: Clarendon Press, 1961.

TRANSNATIONAL MELANCHOLY

RÜDIGER KUNOW

"People between two countries always feel sorrow"[1]: Some Preliminary Reflections on Transnational Affects

It is a truth (almost) universally acknowledged that most people today experience their world as intensely connected—trans-nationally, trans-culturally or in any other way meaningfully addressed by the prefix trans. And more and more people do actually *live* this connectedness: exiles, diasporans, migrants, refugees, all of them positioned in the space of the trans, the ever-tightening network woven by capital-driven globalization. However, both the general public and the academy have so far paid only scant attention to the emotive side of this situation. When the fabric of the customary world in which people have grown up is torn[2] by experiences of displacement, we can plausibly expect that this will provoke intense emotional responses. It is perhaps no co-incidence that at the same time very little is known in any systematic way about the affects developed by people living in the trans, we know more about the sentiments of people in the countries receiving them. There has been widespread talk about globalization *angst* which has indeed become a staple item in the popular press, and is routinely addressed also in academic writing.[3] Yet, *angst*, however "globalized" it may be, clearly does not exhaust the panoply of sentiments awakened, sustained, or repressed in the world of the trans, as more and more people experience the fear of dislocation, homeland nostalgia, job insecurity, environmental risks, to name only a few emotionally charged constellations.

Against this background I will in this paper discuss what social and cultural work is being performed by *affect* in the negotiation and also the critique of transnational social and cultural practices, especially mobility. I seek to show how in the crucible of intense sentiments, the make-up of the individual body as well as that of the body politic are being re-negotiated and re-configured across wide distances and that cultural practices play a crucial role in these processes.

---

1   This phrase is taken from an interview with a Bangla Deshi migrant (qtd. in Gardner 74).
2   I am taking this metaphor from Judith Butler's debate on the purview of post-Foucauldian critique. In this context she says that it is from "the tear in the fabric of our epistemological web, that the practice of critique emerges [...]" (Butler 215).
3   For a recent assessment that tends to downplay disaffection with globalization as a "rich world" phenomenon, see Mark Thirlwell especially pages x, 7, 43.

I.

Much reflection on the transnational condition in the general public and certainly in the academy has been energized by one emblematic figure: the (im)migrant. In her blueprint for transnational cultural critique in American studies Fisher Fishkin has called him and her "proverbial" (24) and in doing so reflected a growing consensus, shared by critics and cultural practitioners alike. A prominent example is Salman Rushdie, for whom "the migrant, the man without frontiers, is the archetypal figure of our age" (Rushdie 414). There is no space here to dwell in detail on the multiplicity of critical inscriptions that this generic figure has received in aesthetic and theoretical contexts. Multiple as they are, these inscriptions, however, tend to gravitate towards one particular perspective: immigrants and migrants more generally are for the most part described as paragons of innovation, examplars of a forward-looking, hands-on subjecthood, forever in search for new opportunities beyond the horizon. Homi Bhabha has been one of the most influential proponents of this view. He has even invested the subject position of migrancy with the aura of the "beyond": "Beyond signifies spatial distance, marks progress, promises the future; [...] The[se] terms that insistently gesture to the beyond, only embrace its restless and revisionary energy if they transform the present into an expanded and ex-centric site of experience and empowerment" (4). In such view, migrants as beings of the "beyond" enact a transgressive and transformational performance in the course of which something new, as Bhabha writes, "begins its presencing" (1). What remains outside the purview of such at times Pollyannaish views of migrancy is the simple fact that—while newness begins its presencing—other things start to "absence" themselves: ties to the homeland, its values and traditions, the security of acquired status and, above all, kinship ties with loved ones left behind. Taken together these absences circumscribe the price to be paid for the enabling prospects of migrancy, a price, moreover, that is exacted more often than not in the currency of feelings, of dejection, despondency, sorrow.

II.

Even while I do not deny that there are indeed individual or local communal euphorias aroused by the unprecedented vistas and possibilities created by the whole new panoply of mobility practices, my focus in the following pages will be more on the so-called "negative" emotions: melancholia, fear, dread, or even panic. Such a choice justifies itself by taking us to a domain that might be called "the second thoughts" which participants in mobility or globalization practices might at one point or other entertain, sentiments coming up during migration or after arrival, at moments when globalized practices and their outcomes have lost their first luster and are coming up for review, for reflection, even self-reflection. What is more, the focus on "second thoughts" allows us to view mobility not as a uni-directional process more or less completed after arrival in another country, but a process that proceeds more like a feedback loop in which various stages or steps are continuously subjected to (self-)review and attendant attitudinal or behavioral modifications.

Reflexivity is here understood along the lines suggested by Ulrich Beck, Anthony Giddens and Scott Lash as a moment of self-critique in times of modernity, as "self-confrontation with the effects" of individual or collective behavior (5). Making this concept work for the present inquiry requires that we scale it down from the level of global social theory to the individual actors and practices the theory seeks to describe. Within this smaller framework, then, I propose that the *moment of self-reflexive confrontation* by the participants with the troubles and setbacks incurred in the world of the trans can be seen as opening up not only a space for intellectual debate, but also for sentiments. And sentiments, especially if they are intensely felt and shared, have historically proven to be effective generators of communication (Ahmed 117). The persons involved in contemporary mobilizations are no exception to this rule.

In order to fit negative emotions into this framework of communicable reflexivity, it is necessary to leave behind the mundane understanding of affects in general (and especially negative ones) as intensely private feelings located deep inside a person. The common phrase "to bear a deep-sitting grudge" against someone or something illustrates this mundane perspective quite nicely because it captures both aspects just mentioned: The "grudge" is here said to be lodged in the inside, even deeply so, *and* to be that person's very own, his or her very own "property." Over against this intuitive "vertical" approach to affects I propose—following recent, especially feminist-inspired research (Ahmed, Wise and Velayutham, Ghandi)—that we look at them in what might be called "horizontal" terms and focus on the *relations* which they (help) configure. Affects situated *in the relations between persons* can be shown to perform intense and effective psychic as well as socio-cultural work. Especially negative ones have historically often provided occasion for re-asserting old and establishing new conceptual binaries around the axis of "them" and "us," inside and outside. Such a resolutely "lateral" reading of affects, as Sara Ahmed has persuasively argued, allows us to understand how affects "align some subjects with some others and against other others [… and] play a crucial role in the 'surfacing' of individual and collective bodies […]" (117). In Ahmed's reading, affects are not an occasional flaring up of sentiments, they—and especially fear and resentment among them—are the very essence of which communities are formed and sustained:

> [F]ear works to secure forms of the collective. My argument therefore is not that there exists a psychic economy of fear that then becomes social and collective: rather, the individual subject comes into being through its very alignment with the collective. It is the very failure of affect to be located in a subject or object that allows it to generate the surfaces of collective bodies. (128)

Ahmed's argument concerning the affective dynamics of fear can be usefully extended to include other emotions as well, including the "negative" affects enumerated above. In this sense, then, I hope to offer some preliminary reflections on how transnational forms of sentiment perform important social and cultural work in our own time by producing affective ties among "globalized" self-critical subjects.

I will trace this production of affective ties among one particular group of migrants: those coming to the U.S. from the Indian subcontinent (Pakistan, India and Bangladesh). While this choice reflects a personal preference and derives from a personal research agenda, there are other and better reasons for it, chief among them that migrants from this part of world are often said to be a "model minority" making the most of the chances offered by immigration. So they are unlikely candidates for entertaining second thoughts, especially negative ones, about their own re-location and even less likely to develop negative sentiments. However, and perhaps surprisingly, there is a large body of recent research about Subcontinental migrants, and here especially non-resident Indians (NRIs) which reveals a "paradoxical mixture of angst and delight, promise and sacrifice" (Lamb 233) among this group. I will trace the contours of this mixture in a number of areas, ranging from the formal to the personal, from the social to the aesthetic.

III.

During the last decade or so, the Indian community in the United States has witnessed a much noted and highly controversial tendency towards increasing support for forms of "transnational centrism" which stabilize the referent "India" around determinately essentialist notions of Pan-Indianness (Bhalla 120). While this is true of NRIs of all backgrounds and ages, studies have shown that it is especially the second-generation of diasporic Indians in America, the ABCDs (American-born confused Deshis), among whom new forms of emotionally charged transnational identity politics are emerging, catalyzed by strong, at times even militant forms of cultural nationalism and radical forms of Hinduism (Kurien, "To be or not to be," 267-269).

On college campuses throughout the United States, Hindu student organizations have declared their support for the cultural politics pursued by the Hindu Student Council (SC), founded in 1990 as a branch of the fundamentalist Vishwa Hindu Parishad, the World Hindu Council. While this development seems to proceed on a par with the turn to religion among cultures throughout the Global North and South, it involves, in this particular case, "religion's becoming an important and emotional part of the personal identity" of young and successful second-generation immigrants (Kurien, "Being Young," 456). Hinduism itself is most often perceived as a pluralistic, syncretistic and tolerant religious belief. However, since the 1970s in India and two decades later in the United States, a fundamentalist version of Hinduism has emerged, organized around the concept of Hindutva. In this perspective, true Indianness rests in the Vedic culture and its sacred texts, dated around 1500 to 1000 years BCE. In the view of Hindutva adherents, this Vedic culture was later eroded and changed almost beyond recognition by various "invader cultures," beginning with the Muslimic Moghuls and ending with the colonizing British. In this fashion, Hindu fundamentalism espouses what is in fact, a pre-national definition of Indianness, and moreover one positioned inside a transnational framework *avant la lettre*.

What is more, Hindutva messages of "Hinduism under siege" are finding more and more support, not, as might be expected, among those that have lost much in the new transnational dispensation but those that seem to profit most from it (Bhalla 120). Religious and cultural nationalism among highly mobile, highly educated and affluent migrants finds its expression in various forms of group activism, ranging from classes in reading the Vedic texts (often in English translation) to performing pujahs (religious observances), to fundamentalist web sites which are at times closed down by web administrators for statements perceived racially offensive (for more material see Bhalla and Kurien).

The "New Indians" (Vibha Bhalla's term) and their affective inscription of the home in terms of "sanatana dharma" (eternal faith) is independent, at times even divorced from, and often in excess of, related practices of Indians in India, it amounts to the creation of an "American Hinduism" directed at the diasporic situation in the United States, not so much in India. Such an adopted identity involves a decided and often emotional rejection also of multiculturalism in the United States and postmodernist notions of flexible non-essentialist selves (Portes 110). Hindutva as a self-identified creed of, by, and for, the Elect, does not espouse the victimization outlook of many other migrant groups in the U.S. Instead, Hindu fundamentalists insist on the pristine purity of their cultural heritage, theirs is a performance of cultural authenticity, not mixture. As one HSC member put it:

> I think it is not doing [our heritage] justice if we assimilate into Western culture, which isn't really a culture. It's a blending of lots of different cultures. If you don't hold onto tradition, it becomes something that the Western media just commercializes. For instance, I find it so sacrilegious to see Ganesha on a T-shirt. (qtd. in Kurien, 450)

Such emotionally charged views (cf. the use of the word "sacrilegious") position themselves at the extreme other end of the notions of Indianness represented by intellectuals of Indian descent such as Bhabha or Rushdie. And while

Rushdie himself has highlighted the fabricated, even ideological status of "Indianness", forms of essentialist Indianness have sought to ground themselves in the "emotional intensities" (Tölölyan qtd. in Werbner 8) of a reconfirmed religious attachment that is exclusive in more senses than one.

IV.

One of the hot spots, the pivotal areas, which tend to galvanize strong sentiments (especially those of loss and longing) is that of intergenerational relations. Most of the migrants in the United States are coming from cultures in which kinship relations play a much stronger role than in their adopted home country. At the same time participation in transnational mobility practices does disperse families, and also the "intimate relationships" (Wald 4) which sustain them. This can be said also for migrants from the Indian Subcontinent, for whom the Indian Extended Family remains a form of life around which emotional and moral intensities have historically always aggregated. Therefore, it is in the framework of intergenerational ties that affects can and do indeed travel long distances, become transnational in their own right.

As Amanda Wise and Selvaraj Velayutham have shown, it is especially cases of non-conformative behavior by younger migrants which, mediated via "the power of gossip, gaze and nandri-kaadan (thankful indebtedness), generate[s] a range of secondary affects such as guilt, shame, fear of ostracism and pride" (4), and does so over long distances. To illustrate this process in which sentiments produce conformity in the transnational arena they tell the story of a young man who, after completing his studies abroad, was expected to return to his village and enter into an arranged marriage to a cousin in the village. However, he began a relationship with a woman from the host country. The couple was spotted and the news of this perceived misalliance quickly reached the home village in India. For the young man's parents this meant shame and social ostracism so that they prevailed on their son to end his relationship. He gave in and married his cousin (ibid.). In order to conceptualize processes such as this, Wise and Velayutham suggest the term "transnational affects" which they hope will help re-orient transnational research to pay greater attention to "the traffic as well as the role of affects and emotion in the reproduction of transnational social fields" (2). Within the compass of the present inquiry it may be interesting to note that they explicitly favor an extension of research such as theirs "to explore in future, the intensities of nostalgic, sensorial and embodied memories" (3).

But even in cases where intergenerational relations are not so spread out over great distances across the transnational canvas, the relations between young and old remain an emotionally charged area. Katy Gardner, in her study of Bangladeshi migrants in London offers interesting empirical material which suggests that highly emotional links between intergenerationality and interculturality exist in the transnational forcefield. In interviews she conducted with aged migrants, these are almost unanimously apprehensive about perceived changes in family and kinship relations that have developed in the wake of their own migration: "We have had our ways since our forefathers: each in turn has provided for the other. But in this country I'm not really providing for my sons, the government is. So they owe me nothing and I can no longer expect anything from them" (Abdullah Ali, Gardner 160). Growing old in a different culture has left its mark on all generations: "Bringing them [our children] here was our ruination. They are ruined. They would recognize me had I not brought them to this country. If they were in Bangladesh they would recognize me" (same interview, 154). The term chosen by the translator, "recognize," in this interview references a whole complex of intergenerational exchanges, forms of respect and attachments and also a culture-specific form of gendered age identity, the murabbi, a highly respected and religiously authorized male elder. Says another migrant: "when we saw a murabbi, we'd never have smoked in front of them. It was considered really insulting to their status. Nowadays though [young people of Bangladeshi descent in Britain] will light up in front of you and push you aside to let them pass" (Abdul Bari, Gardner 153). Intergenerational conflicts arising in the wake of their own migrancy get frequently cited by migrants as cause for a strong sense of disaffection, they are the cause for having second thoughts about the wisdom of their decision to come to the West in the first place. As one elderly woman put it, "[p]eople between two countries always feel sorrow" (Mrs. Khatun, Gardner 74).

V.

Given the salience of strongly felt sentiments in the transnational forcefield, it is no surprise that affects of the kind described here also make their appearance in cultural and mass cultural products. I will refer to just one example, taken from "Bollywood," a summary term for a commercially successful world-wide form of cultural production which has successfully challenged even Hollywood's hegemony. In point of fact, Bollywood has become an indispensible factor in shaping, even producing, high-intensity emotional attachments to "India" among diasporic Indians worldwide.

My example here is "Kal Ho Naa Ho: An Indian Love Story" (KHNH). This film opens with an extended sequence on New York City, one of the prime destinies of migration from the Subcontinent, and it is almost immediately claimed as "Indian" when the voice-over declared that one in four faces in NYC is "Indian." After thus "homeing in" on New York, the film proceeds with a second "homeing in," this time on an extended, multi-generational Indian family who have a hard time making it in the new country. Their diner generates only sluggish business, quite unlike the Chinese restaurant across the street. As they mull over giving up their restaurant, a relative newly arrived from India (Bollywood super star Shhrukh Khan as cousin Aman) has the solution: "We must make use of being Indians. [...] We must get India to New York, spread it in all directions. India can do anything, anytime, anywhere!" This means that they convert the American-style diner into an Indian restaurant, which quickly becomes a veritable bonanza and produces happiness with a sweet tinge of nostalgia among the family till the next vagary of fate strikes them. There is no space here to trace in detail the melodramatic twists and turns of the rest of the film.

Rather, I want to stress that the principal advice propagated here for Indians living abroad is a turn to "India" and her traditions. That these traditions are spurious at times—there is no such thing as Indian food, rather there is a countless variety of regional cuisines and dietary rules—that these traditions may not even exist does not matter. Indian food is functioning here as embodiment of a principle which underwrites so many Bollywood films, the principle of "moving around but keeping India in your heart" (Punathambekar 153, 156). This principle may account for the immense commercial success of this and other such films among NRIs since it sanctions migration, acknowledges the affective deprivations in its wake, *and* offers a solution in terms of a gratification of some form of homeland nostalgia: you can feel at home even abroad. KHNH is thus anything but a case of "cinematic counter-telling," as film critic Ella Shohat calls those productions that attempt to counteract colonialist distortions of "third world identity." I am not suggesting that all Bollywood films featuring diasporic Indians are like this. What I do hope to have shown is how pop cultural representations of the homeland are to no small degree involved in "the business of 'nostalgia economics'" (Rushdie qtd. in Kumar 30).

VII.

Another feature of Subcontinental diasporic culture is Indian literature in English. Aside from the towering figure of Salman Rushdie a large and widely different number of writers, many of them women, has emerged whose fictions zero in on the cultural but also emotional contradictions and ambivalences of "model minority" life in the United States.

My principal example here is Chitra Banerjee Divakaruni whose fictions highlight and elicit more than others an affect-based response to transnational living. In her commercially most successful text, the magically realist *Mistress of Spices* (1997), the eponymous mistress is a healer figure sent by a woman spirit, The Old One, to the United States, to "aid all who come to her in distress" (92)—distress experienced in the aftermath of migration. Battered Subcontinental women, their husbands who have lost their jobs, children of Indian descent mobbed by classmates at school, these and others who are "struck by the sudden vertigo of homelessness" (128) bring their emotional anguish to the spice shop in the Bay Area where the Mistress administers healing with the help of an almost stereotypical staple of the Subcontinent: various condiments.

The enabling proposition of Divakaruni's novel is that Subcontinentals in the U.S. are emotionally deprived, an idea she develops further in the short story "Mrs. Dutta Writes a Letter" (1998)[4]. The letter that the titular figure is planning to write is a letter "home," to an old friend of hers who stayed in India while Mrs. Dutta moved to the United States. This narrative ploy allows Divakaruni to "shadow" her depiction of a materially successful life in the United States with references to what Rushdie called an "imaginary homeland" with its customary ways of life, the homeways that are intensely and nostalgically remembered in flashbacks. The *donné* of the story is a rather recent development in transnational migration which has caught the attention also of anthropologists and cultural critics, the migration of Subcontinental seniors (mostly from India) to the United States and Britain. This relocation late in life occurs most often at the suggestion of the children who after having achieved material prosperity want to have their parents with them and in this way transplant the ideals of the extended family to the adopted country (Lamb 206-234). This is the case also with the fictional Mrs. Dutta who after her husband's death is invited to live with her son Sagar and his family in California who live in a comfortable suburban home with all modern household appliances and even a maid.

However, it is this same material prosperity that takes away much from Mrs. Dutta's traditional way of life, especially her gendered role of caring mother and grandmother, "that sweet, aching urgency of being needed again" (II,5).[5] It is not only the enforced role change that is a constant source of emotional anguish; her grandchildren and to a lesser extent her son and his wife follow their own and very American ways. These ways remain enigmatic to Mrs. Dutta: "Oh, this new country, where all the rules are upside down, it's confusing her" (II,7).

An old friend from India, Mrs. Basu, has written, and the urge to write back is the narrative ploy that precipitates what Beck et al. call "self-confrontation with the effects" of her migration. Mrs. Dutta's taking stock of her situation, her reflections about old vs. new ways, make up the greater part of the story and even bring up occasional moments of self-censorship, as when her "family loyalty battles with insidious feeling of—but she turns from them quickly" (I,2). The story never specifies what Mrs. Dutta's feelings are feelings of. Rather than settling for one particular affect, it offers a veritable panoply of sentiments: "anger," "shame" (I, 3), "disappointment" (I,4), "heartsickness" (I, 5), etc. In the end, after suffering another deeply felt humiliation, this time

---

4   My thanks to Beate Eisner for alerting me to this story.
5   Page references are to the net publication of the story in two parts. The Roman numeral indicates the segment, the second to the page.

from her daughter-in-law, Mrs. Dutta sits down eventually to compose her reply to Mrs. Basu. While suggesting that she may return to India one day, Mrs. Dutta declares, albeit in a qualified way, that she is happy after all: "perhaps, in spite of all that has happened, I am—the happinesss will be in the finding out" (II, 11). However, after thus giving Mrs. Dutta to develop a self-reflective stance toward her experiences, Divakaruni switches tone again, and closes her story on a strongly affective note: "[N]ow that she no longer cares whether tears blotch her letter, she feels no need to weep" (11).

This ending allows Divakaruni to turn the well-worn story format of immigrant fiction into an open-ended *éducation sentimentale*, giving voice to the paradoxical "mixture of nostalgia and resourcefulness" (Lamb 233) in the affective economy of migrants.

VII.

In conclusion, I would like to tabulate a few points and make some suggestions about what the focus on affects in transnational contexts might do for cultural critique. This article develops the concept of transnational affects to argue for the inclusion of sentiments into the cultural critique of globalization and multi-locale forms of living. Over the last decades, we in Cultural studies and also in American studies have been privileging a transnationalism of activities and subversion, without paying much attention to how the people involved in these activities and connections actually feel about them.

However, "a focus on displaced individuals moving through macro-systems involves a much more basic reorientation than extending our ethnographic horizons to more than one locale" (Amit-Talai 330). As they are circulating outside their original cultural entitlements and inflected by transversal and multidirectional movements across and between a variety of geographical and cultural locations, migrants, not only those of Subcontinental descent, become multiply interpellated subjects. Hence, the transnational cultural protocols unfolding inside them do not exhaust themselves in the dialectic of home and away, the *fort-da* of cultural retention and cultural distention.

The focus in transnational analytics on emotions as *moments of self-reflexive confrontation* with the effects of transnational mobility furthermore marks a whole set of conceptual failures, of identity, transformation, mobility, home, etc., while at the same time describing emergent forms of more *intimate connectivities* inside what Hardt and Negri call the "decentered and deterritorializing apparatus" (xii) of capitalist globalization.

What is more, the emotional intensities among out-of-place people and the respected objects and situations around which they aggregate tend to vary considerably. Emotions may travel transnationally over long distance but that does not mean that they are also transcultural. Rather, given the salience of kinship and especially intergenerational relations, it is quite plausible that future research on transnational affects will find much usefully material in this field. However that may be, I want to close by suggesting that transnational affects will allow us to move conceptually from mobility in the abstract to concrete constellation which are multi-locale *and* nested, to zones of comfort and discomfort, in which transnational dynamics are invested with personal, at times even intimate meaning.

Works Cited

Ahmed, Sara. "Affective Economies." *Social Text* 22:2 (2004): 117-139.

Amit-Talai, Vered. "In precarious motion: from territorial to transnational cultures." *The Canadian Review of Sociology and Anthropology* 34 ,3 (1997): 319-332.

Beck, Ulrich, Anthony Giddens and Scott Lash. *Reflexive Modernization: Politics, Tradition and Aesthetics in the Modern Social Order*. Ed. Beck, Giddens and Lash. Stanford: Stanford UP, 1994.

Bhabha, Homi K. *The Location of Culture.* London: Routledge, 1994.

Bhalla, Vibha. "The New Indians: Reconstructing Indian Identity in the United States." *American Behavioral Scientist* 50, 1 (2006): 118-136.

Butler, Judith. "What is Critique? An Essay on Foucault's Virtue." *Political Readings in Continental Philosophy.* Ed. David Ingram. Oxford: Blackwell, 2002. 212-228.

Divakaruni, Chitra Banerjee. *The Mistress of Spices.* London: Black Swan, 1997.

---. "Mrs. Dutta Writes a Letter." *The Atlantic Monthly* 281, 4 (1998): 88-97; rpt. www.theatlantic.com/past/docs/issues/98apr/dutta2.htm; accessed 14 September 2011.

Fisher Fishkin, Sally. "Crossroads of Cultures: The Transnational Turn in American Studies—Presidential Address to the American Studies Association, November 12, 2004." *American Quarterly* 57, 1 (2005): 17-57.

Gardner, Katy. *Age, Narrative and Migration: The Life Course and Life Histories of Bengali Elders in London*. Oxford: Berg, 2002.

Ghandi, Leela. *Affective Communities: Anticolonial Thought, Fin-de-Siècle Radicalism, and the Politics of Friendship.* Durham: Duke University Press, 2006.

Hardt, Michael, and Antonio Negri. *Empire.* Cambridge: Harvard University Press, 2000.

Kal Ho Naa Ho: Indian Love Story. Dir. Nikhil Advani. Perf. Shah Ruhk Khan, Preity Zinta, Sushma Seth. Rapid Eye Movies, 2003. Film.

Kumar, Amitava. *Bombay – London – New York*. New York: Routledge, 2002.

Kurien, Prema. "To Be or Not to Be South Asian: Contemporary Indian American Identity Politics." *Journal of Asian American Studies* 6, 3 (2003): 261-288.

---. "Being Young, Brown, and Hindu: The Identity Struggles of Second-Generation Indian Americans." *Journal of Contemporary Ethnography* 34, 4 (2005): 434-469.

Lamb, Sarah. *Aging and the Indian Diaspora: Contemporary Families in India and Abroad*. Bloomington: Indiana University Press, 2009.

Portes, Alejandro, and Ruben G. Rumbaut. *Legacies: The story of the immigrant second-generation*. Berkeley: University of California Press, 2001.

Punathambekar, Aswin. "Bollywood in the Indian American Diaspora: Mediating a Transitive Cultural Citizenship." *International Journal of Cultural Studies* 8, 2 (2005): 151-173.

Rushdie, Salman. "Step Across this Line." *Step Across this Line: Collected Non-Fiction*. London: Jonathan Cape, 2002. 407-442.

Thirlwell, Mark. "Second Thoughts on Globalization: Can the developed world cope with the rise of China and India?" *Lowy Institute Paper* 18. Double Bay: Longueville, 2007.

Wald, Priscilla. *Contagious: Cultures, Carriers and the Outbreak Narrative*. Durham: Duke UP, 2008.

Werbner, Pnina. *Imagined Diasporas among Manchester Muslims: The Public Performance of Pakistani Transnational Identity Politics*. Santa Fe: School of American Research Press, 2002.

Wise, Amanda, and Selvaraj Velayutham. "Towards a Typology of Transnational Affect." Centre for Research on Social Inclusion, Working Paper No. 4. Sidney: Macquarie University, 2006; www.crsi.mq.edu.au; accessed 15 March 2011.

ANTONIA MEHNERT

"Ou libéré?"—Transnational Trauma in *Breath, Eyes, Memory* by Edwidge Danticat

I. Introduction

While in the age of globalization we are experiencing an increase in transnational mobility and facilitated ways of communication seemingly connect people around the globe, the negative effects of these dynamics often remain unacknowledged. Literary and cultural critics praise the opportunities resulting from global networks and point to the empowerment and possibilities, especially for minorities, to write against dominant discourses as national boundaries lose their importance and center-margin dichotomies seem no longer at work (see Bhabha, de Toro). Furthermore, studies in the Humanities in the past two decades revolved around the discussion of identity formation in a transnational context, emphasizing identity's performative and pluralistic nature while distancing themselves from a holistic perception of cultures.[1] Most of these works then focus extensively on minority groups and call for a visibility of "difference" in society and thus an inclusion of identities formerly silenced. It is foremost an attempt of subaltern groups to fill the blank spaces of (trans-) national geography, to inscribe their presence into the dominant discourses and to thereby defy an imposed definition of self from the outside.

However, many theoretical discussions fail to take a closer look at the other, more hidden, side of the migrant experience which is often marked by painful events and demonstrates that while resisting outer identification, the acceptance of the "Other" within the self and one's own fragmented identity, becomes sometimes unbearable for the individual. Especially in an US-Caribbean context the multi-positionality of cultural identity is prominent, but is not necessarily portrayed positively, as some novels by US-Caribbean authors demonstrate. Works such as *Breath, Eyes, Memory* by Edwidge Danticat, which will be the subject of discussion in this article, but also others such as *Drown* by Junot Diaz or *Lucy* by Jamaica Kincaid, expose the downsides of mobility, diaspora and the resulting in-betweenness in order to "recover the political meanings and subaltern agency that have been barred entry by the free-floating gatekeeper of global theory" (Sheller in Donnell 86) and its positive portrayal of borderlessness.

---

1 See also Glissant's *Poetics of Relation*, "in which each and every identity is extended through a relationship with the Other" (Glissant 11) which also elaborates on Deleuze and Guattari's idea of the rhizome.

Even though, these authors come from very different parts of the Caribbean, they do share a similar experience: their islands have all experienced colonial oppression and later US-political intervention and all of them live now outside their home (-islands). As Lahens explains, "colonial zeal and its national prolongation have thus made the writer a foreigner in his own country and perhaps simply foreign, the very prototype of the modern nomad" (151). This has influenced their literary works in different ways, identity being a central common point and the discussion of "its (de) formation within (post/neo) colonial/patriarchal contexts" (Adjarian 4). Coming along with this deformation and also being a reason for it, are the often formerly experienced traumas. Generally defined as experiences of an overwhelming and catastrophic set of events (Caruth), which in the actual moment of intrusion cannot be grappled with or understood, they repeatedly show different symptoms afterwards. Many events in US-Caribbean history can thus be considered potential causes for traumatic experiences—the often violently employed practices of neo-colonialism just serving as one example.

For a more critical discussion of postcolonial literature, it may be productive to take a closer look at the literary portrayal of the exiled and traumatized bodies and its effects on identity construction. It is furthermore through the literature of authors such as Edwidge Danticat and her "insistence on confronting the violence, terror and despair Haitians face as well as her keen understanding of the myriad ways in which they attempt to transcend their fears and consequent paranoia through an imaginative realm" (Clitandre 226) that one becomes conscious of the possible adversities involved in a life in exile.

II. Narrating Trauma

Many of these Caribbean authors, trauma victims or not, engage in a critical dialogue with history and point to psychological effects of colonialism while portraying the neglect and disempowerment of marginalized individuals today. The narrations furthermore explore trauma as a multicontextual social issue instead of presenting it as a pure psychological subject and raise questions about collective memory and its representation of personal traumatic histories. Fragmented identities, dissociation and emotions further influence the remembering of trauma and provide the reader with a rather partial but empathic understanding of theses (hi)stories. This affect can be essential to understanding historical phenomena and to better comprehend the individual experience of a historical traumatic event. Vickroy explains that,

> trauma narrativists' endeavor to expand their audiences' awareness of trauma by engaging them with personalized, experientially oriented means of narration that highlight the painful ambivalence that characterizes traumatic memory and warn us that trauma reproduces itself if left unattended. (3)

When trauma is accepted as a social problem, because it is considered in a broader context and readers become witnesses of formerly unknown histories, victims of trauma cannot only find the necessary social surrounding that enables healing, but they can also emerge from their stigmatized position in society (see also Herman, Caruth). Trauma specialist Kali Tal criticizes the US strategy of neglecting trauma victims—often poor, marginalized—in order to maintain a certain "healthy" image of the nation. She furthermore examines the relationship between individual trauma and cultural representations of the traumatic event and portrays that "when traumatic stories are told and retold, they enter the vocabulary of the larger culture and become tools for the construction of national and cultural myths" (1). Trauma narratives thus offer a way for groups to (re)inscribe themselves into larger *imagined communities* (Anderson) and permit for cultural memory to be revaluated. Vickroy furthermore explains, "knowledge of trauma offers the opportunity to unveil new perspectives concerning relationships of power and their effects, to analyze what we repress and why, and to examine our need for cultural and individual myths that block understanding" (22).

One of the fundamental questions in trauma studies is: How can trauma be communicated? The body hereby takes on a central position. It constitutes one of the sites where the traumatic effects of history are inscribed and it sometimes becomes the only outlet and witness for the usually repressed traumatic experience and of stories otherwise muted. Lionett explains,

> [a]s a canvas upon which historical problems of domination and physical or verbal violence, either latent or manifest, are sketched out, the body now reflects the strategic choices forced upon the alienated and colonized subjects, who want to be "other," and who search for themselves in other lands. (34)

While this quote portrays that the body records historical events, it also alludes to the many reasons for traumatization, such as colonialism, its aftermath and today's political oppression. In order to overcome the fragmentary and alienated sense of self resulting from these experiences, the characters in the novel *Breath, Eyes, Memory* seek wholeness of their bodies in other countries (either the US or through the return to the home country)—not always with success. By focusing on the vulnerability of the body, the author Edwidge Danticat critically portrays how its function is often claimed by the people in power and how certain positions are ascribed to it. Di Prete further elaborates:

> [T]he body enters representation always as a sign (the "sema") through which a given culture negotiates and consolidates hegemonic values, norms, and beliefs. In the shift into representation, the material, physical body with its distinctive traits ("soma") becomes displaced through the cultural and ideological content that is attached to it" (14).

While the characters in the novels suffer from this imposition of meaning because it determines their existence on the margins of society, their bodies speak out the cruelties inflicted upon them and attempt to resist further definition from the outside. Hence the quest for the "wholeness" of the body, and thus its healing of the psychosomatic effects of trauma, becomes a struggle for self-empowerment and self-expression.

In the following more detailed analysis of Danticat's novel *Breath, Eyes, Memory* I will show that bodies not only account for violent historical processes but also become the sites of a *transnational* trauma. The fact that the characters are not necessarily free in their "new" surroundings, but are haunted by the ghosts of the past, demonstrates that the traumatic experience is at the base of the transnational. Memory and dealing with the trauma explicitly, however, can lead to personal recovery. I furthermore argue that Danticat finally writes against a cultural amnesia, which postulates one "healthy" cultural memory and denies the existence of personal traumatic experiences. Through the inscription of the characters' personal trauma in the novel she "create(s) alternative histories from the perspectives of individuals formerly silenced" (Vickroy 38).

III. Transnational Traumas in *Breath, Eyes, Memory*

As a writer in exile, Danticat, who was born in Haiti in 1969 and moved to the US at the age of 12, puts herself not only in the tradition of the storytellers of her home country but also attempts to describe what has remained unrecorded by history textbooks so far. Even though her work *Breath, Eyes, Memory* is explicitly a work of fiction, as the subtitle "a novel" demonstrates, it incorporates autobiographical elements, as well as certain historical reference points and can also be read as a testimonial for its engagement in witnessing the violence or social injustice inflicted on the subaltern. By incorporating migrant stories and oral histories formerly unknown, Danticat creates "the discourse of the possible rather than the (purported) actual, [and] offers a way to both remember what history neglects and resets the terms of what gets judged as (historically) significant" (Adjarian 114). Fiction does then no longer rely on the history of the dominant culture, whose focus has been on the larger events in national-historical discourse in order to construct meaning, but rather it gives space to the "living memories of the past" (Danticat 56).

The novel depicts the painful female history of three generations of a Haitian family. The story begins with the departure of Sophie who, after twelve years of separation, is forced to move to New York to be reunited with her mother. This, however, is not a long hoped-for reunion in the eyes of Sophie but means an unwanted separation from her aunt who has raised her like her own child. Even though her neighbors consider it "the best thing that is ever going to happen to [her]" (Danticat 14), Sophie is afraid of missing Tante Atie so much that she could die of *chagrin*, which is according to her aunt "not a sudden illness, but something that could kill you slowly, taking a small piece of you every day until one day it finally takes all of you away" (Danticat 25). This sense of homesickness plays a crucial role throughout the entire novel: it describes the continuous suffering in the search of something or someone intangible and at the same time it implies that the (e)motion devours you until you do not exist anymore. Historically read, *chagrin* is the painful experience of Haitian women who have seen the deaths of their husbands in battlefields, at the hand of dictators or during the exhausting work in the sugarcane fields. It expresses the endless unfulfilled hope for wholeness or belonging. This scene also implies that homelessness leads ultimately to psychological damage because the homesickness evoked by the displacement can destroy you.

Another painful experience expressed in this passage is the unfulfilled yearning for a mother. Colonial history and today's migration have complicated mother-daughter relationships and have often left children behind as orphans. The term orphan proposes a sense of being alone and abandoned, whereas the opposite is hoped for: the desire of being part of something larger than just the individual, of having a home. As explained in *Breath, Eyes, Memory* "your mother is your first friend" (24), but in Haiti "there are many good reasons for mothers to abandon their children" (ibid.). This paradoxical constellation of the close and at the same time abandoning relationship between mother and daughter is one of the reasons for the psychological instability of the female characters in Danticat's novel. For Sophie her aunt has become her mother and she expresses this by giving her a mother's day card. This passage critically questions "in what ways adoption simultaneously disrupt[s] and affirm[s] the fixity of identities and the nurturing roles of women" (Clitandre 235). The confusion of mother roles is not only one of the outcomes of contemporary migratory movements, but carries its roots in the colonial conquests where the colonial mother country was supposed to replace the Caribbean mother country. This confusion of mother roles has left behind "orphans" suffering from a "fundamental loss of security and belonging" (Mahlis 1) all over the Caribbean.

Sophie's sense of belonging is further questioned upon arrival in the US and the reader becomes aware of the drastic influence that migration and separation have on familial relationships as well as on the individual (dis)position. As Laura Vickroy has pointed out in her study on trauma and literature in contemporary fiction, characters suffer from the trauma of the "fragmenting experience of migration and having to re-create one's self in a new context" (64). This 'self-creation' is extremely difficult since the new surrounding is hostile towards Haitian immigrants—an experience that Sophie is also making at school, where she is confronted with the cliché of many American kids that accuse Haitians of having AIDS because they had heard on television that only the '"Four Hs" got AIDS: Heroin addicts, Hemophiliacs, Homosexuals, and Haitians" (Danticat 51). Sophie's mother forces her to learn English as quickly as possible and thus Sophie spends six years doing nothing but studying, praying and being isolated at home, unable to revise the other students' vision who called "[her and her friends] 'boat people' and 'stinking Haitians'" (Danticat 66). Without having a social network, she nevertheless wants to fit in and tries to get rid off her Creole accent, because she is ashamed that her first English words sound like "rocks falling into a stream" (Danticat 66). While Sophie is trying to cope with her new surroundings and to overcome her own trauma of exile and of "orphanage", she comes to realize that her mother Martine is "challenging the tyranny of the past" (Vickroy 64) as well.

Martine was raped by a *Tonton Macoute* during the Duvalier regime and became pregnant with Sophie. She continued to be haunted by the memory of this traumatic experience, of "a man with no face, pounding a life into a helpless young girl" (Danticat 193) and left Haiti and her daughter in the hope to regain mental stability. In the US she is left alone, without a mother and a daughter (again), alone with herself and her memories. Even though she builds a new life, works hard and partially frees herself from patriarchal structures on the island by dating an upper-class Haitian immigrant on her own terms, she cannot overcome her trauma. When Sophie sees her for the first time, her physical appearance mirrors her terrible psychological condition:

> Her face was long and hollow. Her hair had a blunt cut and she had long spindly legs. She had dark circles under her eyes and, as she smiled, lines of wrinkles tightened her expression. Her fingers were scarred and sunburned. It was as though she had never stopped working in the cane fields after all. (Danticat 42)

This description presents a picture of a woman who suffers from insomnia and who seems to be worn out and overworked. It is precisely Sophie's comment on the cane fields, the place where Martine was raped, that brings the past to the present and illustrates that "clearly, [Martine's] years in Haiti and the terrors there dominated her life more than her current environment" (Vickroy 67). At the same time, this description from the novel shows that the continuous suffering of her family in the cane fields is manifested over generations and does not stop at national borders.

Already during the first night Sophie finds out that her mother is suffering from terrible nightmares but Martine cannot yet "speak out" what it is that makes her scream and pound herself at night, instead she insists, "I will be fine. I always am. The nightmares, they come and go" (Danticat 48). This key scene is repeated throughout the novel and it becomes clear that Martine suffers from post-traumatic stress disorder (PTSD). According to Judith Herman, trauma is caused by a "threat to life or bodily integrity, or a close personal encounter with violence or death" (6) that often triggers in the victims a will to forget the traumatic event because of the impossibility of speaking the trauma.[2] This self-

---

2   Granofsky defines PTSD as a problem that results from "a psychologically distressing event that is outside the range of usual human experience" and that is usually accompanied by "intense fear, terror, and helplessness" (10).

protective response to repress the memories because there is no way of integrating the trauma into her life, however, does not lead to recovery; instead, the memories find an outlet in bodily symptoms, such as insomnia, self-straining, beginning anorexia nervosa and finally cancer.

The fact that the traumatic event took place on the island and continues to haunt Martine in the US illustrates that trauma can travel. It shows that the "repercussions of traumatic events in Haiti are psychologically, physically, and cognitively reexperienced in the Diaspora" (Suárez 76). Even though Martine enjoys the new reconnection with her past, that is to say her reunion with her daughter, she cannot hide the traumatic connection that the sight of Sophie's face evokes: "I never saw his face. He had it covered when he did this to me. But now when I look at your face I think it is true what they say. A child out of wedlock always looks like its father" (Danticat 61). Nevertheless, she states this without any sign of emotion, "like naming a color or calling a name. Something that already existed and could not be changed" (Danticat 61). In studies of PTSD it has been pointed out that symptoms also include "feelings of detachment and social estrangement characterized by a markedly reduced ability to feel emotions" (Henke xvi). Similarly, Martine cannot 'feel' the rape again. This repression of the actual event derives from the nature of trauma in the form of belatedness and not immediately knowing what is happening. As Horvitz explains, "the breach in the mind - the conscious awareness of the threat to life - is not caused by a pure quantity of stimulus, but by the lack of preparedness to take in a stimulus that comes too quickly," (62) and this is why the trauma often shows its symptoms later on. This is also why trauma includes a paradox: The experience of a violent event does not coincide with the ability to know it and thus the immediacy transforms into belatedness (Horvitz). Thus, the mind cannot cope with the experience and it appears again and again in the subconscious and Martine's dreams: "Shortly after she fell asleep, I would hear her screaming for someone to leave her alone. I would run over and shake her as she thrashed about. Her reaction was always the same. When she saw my face, she looked even more frightened" (Sophie in Danticat 81). For Martine her daughter takes on the face of her torturer and thus becomes the traumatic living memory of the past.

Paradoxically, the rape ended another traumatic episode in Martine's life: the patriarchal tradition of keeping women "pure" until their marriage - the testing of virginity. It is this obsession with virginity that leads to a violation of the daughter by the mother. Families absorb the repressive practices of Haiti's political regimes and their misogynist practices, and thereby pass on legacies of trauma (see Vickroy) even within a new national context: Martine does not stop the testing practices in the diaspora and instead, trauma 'travels' in the disguise of tradition. The difficult mother-daughter relationship is again presented here as the source of trauma as "mothers denied power overcompensate with futile assertions of control that, for very different reasons but following patterned learned responses, deny their children's difference" (Vickroy 48). Thus, when Sophie falls in love with the significantly older Afro-American musician Joseph from Louisiana, her mother starts to "test" her according to Haitian tradition to ensure that she is still a virgin. Sophie cannot stand this continuous intrusion into her intimacy any longer and deliberately breaks her hymen with a pestle from the kitchen. This set of events determines "Sophie's own difficulty with her body, her sexuality, and her sense of value in the world, her community, and her family" (Suárez 82). Both women believe that one traumatic event is overcome with a forceful intrusion into her body, but it is only the continuation of the transgenerational trauma.

IV. Bodily Inscriptions

The diverse traumatic sets of events that influence the lives of Sophie and Martine make it evident that trauma and body cannot be separated since it is the body that becomes the actual site of the (trans-)national trauma. As feminist literary critic Susan Bordo has pointed out, "the body is a surface on which the central rules, hierarchies and even metaphysical commitments of a culture are inscribed and thus reinforced through the concrete language of the body" (Bordo in Francis). This idea accords also with theories of *performativity* by Judith Butler (1993) which understand the body as a constructed entity that does not exist a priori but is constituted in a continuous negotiation with its environment. The body then becomes the trace from which to search meaning.

In trauma studies it has been explicitly pointed to the crucial importance of bodily inscriptions of trauma. As Horvitz explains, "echoing in the victim's mind, intermingled with her everyday thoughts, the memories turn up in the form of symptoms, including anxiety, depression, and 'conversion symptoms,' wherein psychological pain is converted into physiological disorders, just as it was in hysteria a century ago" (17). These conversion reactions become the body's way of remembering trauma. Thus it is the body where the trauma is engraved and at the same time communicated. At this point, I will return to the testing scene already discussed above, in order to analyze it more in depth, putting emphasis on the bodily inscription of trauma. The patriarchal tradition of testing, in order to keep the virgin body "whole" until marriage, inflicts on the characters physiological and psychological damage. The moment of private intrusion by the mother, who represents a figure of trust, resembles Sophie's final disillusionment of not connecting with her long-lost mother. While she does not yet realize that Martine fulfills this tradition as a way of reclaiming her "own once-intact body and mind" (Vickroy 68), she feels deceived and abused. The violation of Sophie by her mother through the testings furthermore leaves her in a state of profound emptiness: "I was feeling alone and lost, like there was no longer any reason for me to live" (Danticat 87). This state of complete desperation gives her the strength to inflict terrible pain on herself so that her mother's abuse will stop:

> My flesh ripped apart as I pressed the pestle into it. I could see the blood slowly dripping onto the bed sheet. I took the pestle and the bloody sheet and stuffed them into a bag. It was gone, the veil that always held my mother's finger back every time she *tested* me. My body was quivering when my mother walked into my room to test me. My legs were limp when she drew them aside. I ached so hard I could hardly move. Finally I failed the test. (Danticat 88)

However, this self-violation cannot 'free' Sophie but rather results in the continuation of pain. Though physically separated from her mother, Sophie cannot escape her: she continues to be haunted by her mother's imposed suffering. She recalls the moments of testing as well as the images of her mother's nightmares over and over again. Her subsequent bulimia, the sexual problems with her husband and the general sense of being lost evoke a need in her to return to Haiti. On the island, Sophie learns from her grandmother that the practice of testing is the cause for transgenerational pain and is deeply rooted in *machistic* structures of Haitian culture but she, in contrast to her mother, is able to voice its traumatic effects on her body: "I call it humiliation […] I hate my body. I am ashamed to show it to anybody, including my husband. Sometimes I feel like I should be off somewhere by myself. That is why I am here" (Danticat 123).

Sophie's self-violation now stops her from feeling pleasure when she has sex with her husband. Instead, she 'doubles', just like she did before during the testings. Vickroy explains that "splitting off from one's body or awareness can reduce the victim's immediate sense of violation and help them to endure and survive the situation" (13). Sophie's doubling then is the evidence for her critical psychological state of dissociation (Francis): In her imagination she moves to a space of well-being and leaves her body. In order to regain the power of her body after the act, Sophie eats as much as she can, just to purge it all from her body shortly after. Eating numbs her pain and at the same time enables her to cope with the bodily violations. It becomes a way to exercise control over her life. Her pregnancy increases Sophie's discomfort with her body and "even though so much time had passed since [she]'d given birth, [she] still felt extremely fat" (Danticat 112) and is "too ashamed of the stitches on [her] stomach and the flabs of fat all over [her] body" (Danticat 129). Ultimately, Sophie, unable to accept her own appearance which represents at the same time a constant reminder of her mother's rapist, hopes to find answers to help her overcome her bulimia in Haiti, to complete her "Narcissus's yearning for a reflection or identity that will restore her sense of wholeness" (Mardorossian 129). She searches for ways to make her body—which has become foreign and alien through the traumatic experience—familiar again.

Reconciled with Martine, who has also come to the island, the mother confesses to her that she is pregnant again. This new pregnancy, however, cannot revive a body that is already suffering from other illnesses. As cancer is eating away at her (she has already had two mastectomies) and she is rapidly losing weight, the new life inside her poses a new/old threat. Her body, bereft of breasts for nurturing a child, already foreshadows the following set of events. The nightmares of the faceless rapist come back stronger than ever before as past and present, reality and imagination start to blur. Martine begins to see the *violeur* everywhere around her. During her last visit, Martine speaks repeatedly to her daughter about an abortion, because she hears the baby talk to her, "he calls me a filthy whore. I never want to see this child's face" (Danticat 217). Finally, Martine cannot stand this repeated confrontation with the experience of trauma, and she kills herself with 17 stabs in the stomach. As Horvitz explains, "[f]or consciousness then, the act of survival, as the experience of trauma, is the repeated confrontation with the necessity and impossibility of grasping the threat to one's own life. It is because the mind cannot confront the possibility of its death directly that survival becomes for the human being, paradoxically, an endless testimony to the *impossibility of living*" (62, emphasis added). Just like Martine tried to destroy Sophie in her stomach as well as later in person (through the testing), she tries it again with the new baby and this time succeeds while at the same time killing herself.

Taking her own life resembles in this moment paradoxically her survival, because it represents the liberation from the lifelong experience of trauma that she could not verbalize before. The body thus, "violated, abused, and discarded is believed to hold in its factuality a privileged position as the extreme witness of what has happened, right when the subject might be forced into silence by the encounter with an overwhelming experience" (Di Prete 13). The dead body thus serves as a visible reminder for Martine's inability to deal with the trauma. It tells the story of violation while taking on a form of rebellion and liberation since now the trauma can be spoken through the body. *Breath, Eyes, Memory* thus illustrates the "indissoluble bond between voice and body, trauma and corporeality" (Di Prete 2), because through the body of the characters the transgenerational, and transnational trauma manifests itself and serves as a record for the many intrusions in the personal lives in Haitian-American history.

V. Ou libéré? Ways of liberation in *Breath, Eyes, Memory*

Ou libéré? The question of "are you free?" is a recurring motif in the novel and despite the focus on trauma and its bodily inscriptions, there are, however, several strategies and attempts of (self-)liberation in *Breath, Eyes, Memory* which present ways of finding a voice. Whereas Martine at first believes that she can escape the trauma by leaving Haiti, she does not find comfort in the diaspora as there is no help for her to cope with her trauma there either. There is no solidarity that could ease her pain and so she remains a victim in private.[3] Sophie, on the contrary, creates her own safe spaces in the form of doubling and later therapy. In doubling she can finally be at peace with her mother and fulfill the voodoo idea of the two *Marassas*[4]. The powerful image in the story of the daughter being the only person in the world who will not leave the mother provides both with the sense of belonging that is so crucial in order to overcome trauma. In the doubling "we were both safe. The past was gone" (Danticat 200). Even though this quote implies the forgetting of the past, it is at the same time the act of imagination, of making the story of the *Marassas* present, that becomes a necessity for the survival of the traumatic experience. This paradox then proposes that both, remembering and forgetting, are essential to survive and thus it implies that Danticat's larger project of rewriting an alternative memory is not only a process of remembering but also of forgetting.

Sophie becomes ultimately only free because she deals with the trauma – partly because she joins a therapy group. There she learns that her sexual trauma is part of a violent experience shared by women around the world: the Ethiopian college student who had "her clitoris cut and her labia sewn up when she was a girl" (Danticat 201) as well as the Chicana who was raped by her grandfather. Coming from different countries, but now united in their destiny in the US, they all have experienced traumatic violations of their bodies, which now impede them to feel at ease with their sex and sexuality. This transnational trauma group then illustrates that,

> [t]he lives of natives, migrants, refugees, and repatriates are interconnected not only by the global system that links people, places, cultures and objects through displacement and movement, but also by the physical and psychological violence and desperation that moves with them. (Clitandre 226-7)

The group plays such a crucial role because "to hold traumatic reality in consciousness requires a social context that affirms and protects the victim and joins the victim and witness in a common alliance" (Herman 9). It is the belief in survival and the belief in sharing the pain with others that helps the women in the therapy group to overcome their transnational trauma. The group then provides the necessary social context, referred to by Herman, in which the pain can be verbalized. The theory that Horvitz, Cathy Caruth, and others develop, promotes the need for trauma to be spoken and listened to as an articulation of the suffering, violation and disorders, but also to tell it to someone who listens.

---

3   Suárez explains that "before the late eighties, insufficient attention was given to rape victims in the United States and even less to rape victims who had migrated with post-traumatic symptoms from rape" (86).
4   "The *Marassas* were two inseparable lovers. They were the same person, duplicated in two [....]. The love between a mother and a daughter is deeper than the sea. You and I we could be like *Marrasas*" (Danticat 85).

Furthermore, Sophie realizes that it is all part of a transgenerational story of trauma—a vicious circle of endless reproduction of the story—that has to be broken:

> I felt broken at the end of the meeting, but a little closer to being free. I didn't feel guilty about burning my mother's name anymore. I knew my hurtings and hers were links in a long chain and if she hurt me, it was because she was hurt, too. It was up to me to avoid my turn in the fire. It was up to me to make sure that my daughter never slept with ghosts, never lived with nightmares, and never had *her* name burnt in the flames. (Danticat 203)

Therefore, in the end Sophie follows the advice of her therapist to return to Haiti in order to free her mother and herself and leave the ghosts of the past behind. She moreover dresses Martine in red at the funeral even though she knows that it is "too loud a color for burial" (Danticat 227). It is a way of re-creating her mother for "she would look like a Jezebel, hot-blooded Erzulie who feared no men, but rather made them her slaves, raped *them*, and killed *them*" (Danticat 227) and thus making her like Sophie had always imagined her: a strong woman, superior to men. Thereby she repeats the expression that the color is too loud and thus emphasizes the way that women are silenced by the material and cultural forces that restrict them (Scott 475). In a final confrontation with the sugarcane fields, the origin of all family (and historical) trauma, Sophie finds the answer to the question that Grandma Ifé poses:

> There is a place where women are buried in clothes the color of flames, where we drop coffee on the ground for those who went ahead, where the daughter is never fully a woman until her mother has passed on before her. There is always a place where, if you listen closely in the night, you will hear your mother telling a story and at the end of the tale, she will ask you this question. 'Ou libéré?' Are you free my daughter? (Danticat 234)

Sophie understands that she is free despite the fact that the history of the mother will always also be the history of the daughter as implied by the quotation. In her memory she will always carry on the traumatic history of her mother, but it is a reconfigured memory which permits Sophie to reinterpret the traditions of the past and therefore to move on. Thus, her trip to Haiti "functions as a rite of passage that affords closure, privileged knowledge, and enlightenment" (Goldman 162) and enables Sophie to re-member her past without nightmares. Nesbitt explains that the recognition takes place "in the haunting of the present by the past, in which subjects are enchained to their memories, that freedom might be recovered" (212). This passage shows that finally trauma, body and memory are inevitably connected and determine one another. The personal stories that emerge out of this interrelated and mutually conditional network prove histories formerly silenced by the dominant discourse. At the final point of rest in Haiti, Sophie's newly gained freedom becomes a trope for individual power and personal recovery. She is coming to voice.

VI. Conclusion

> To the brave women of Haiti,
> grandmothers, mothers, aunts, sisters, cousins, daughters, and friends,
> on this shore and other shores.
> We have stumbled but we will not fall (Danticat)

This epigraph and dedication highlights the responsibility of the author towards oppressed groups of women around the world. It is a call for survival and a claim for their visibility. In this context, the work of the writer has the potential to reclaim the history of these women and to revise former traditions and cultural memory. Characters and writers alike "use the subconscious, or dreams as symbols for women's subversive potential, as visions that can transform their claustrophobic and often violent lives" (Chancy 230). Personal memories influence these forms of imagination and thereby write histories different from the ones found in textbooks so that the story of the Haitian diaspora can find its place in US cultural memory. As Foucault has pointed out, people barred from writing, from producing their own books had their way of transmitting their own historical accounts through storytelling or songs. He discusses how memory is always an important factor in struggle, and whoever controls people's memory, controls their dynamism. This is why it is important for writers such as Danticat to revise cultural memory and thus change attitudes towards those formerly forgotten. Furthermore, her work counters the idea that societies only remember what is important for their present needs.

In order to successfully integrate these 'other' histories, the novel presents trauma and images of sick and dying bodies to encourage emphatic identification with the suffering "instead of using them to establish Haiti's irredeemable alterity" (Scott). This identification then creates a surrounding in which the voice is heard. The portrayal of a trauma that can travel is crucial to avoid an interpretation that explains the traumatized bodies only in a national and 'Third World' context. The traumatic experience is at the basis of the transnational and by putting the body into the center of the discussion, it makes the reader conscious of the "vulnerability of the material body to the forces of symbolic power" (Ferrari 2) and also shows in what ways the body can reflect past and present events. In the end, Danticat breaks the pattern of bodily definition from the outside (especially in (neo-)colonial contexts) as her character Sophie finds a way to overcome the transhistorical, transnational trauma. The voice that emerges in the healing process needs to be heard in the US as well as in Haiti because it reveals memories that cannot be located in national terms.

Even though trauma studies have pointed to the impossibility of representing the traumatic event in any artistic way "without reconstructing that, which cannot be reproduced" (Suárez 76), it is, nevertheless, necessary for the survival of the victims to create a community of awareness for their trauma. Literature presents this neutral, though public, space where the victim can break the silence and find recovery from pain.[5] Danticat thus puts herself in a tradition of young US-Caribbean writers with a clear political message by giving a voice to formerly unspeakable traumatic histories.

Works Cited

Adjarian, M. M. *Allegories of Desire: Body, Nation, and Empire in Modern Caribbean Literature by Women*. Westport, Conn.: Praeger, 2004.
Anderson, Benedict R. *Imagined Communities: Reflections on the Origin and Spread of Nationalism*. London, 2003.
Bhabha, Homi K. *The Location of Culture*. London: Routledge, 1994.
Butler, Judith. *Bodies that Matter*. London/New York: Routledge, 1993.
Caruth, Cathy. *Unclaimed Experience*. Baltimore: The John Hopkins UP, 1996.
Chancy, Myriam. *Searching for Safe Spaces*. Philadelphia: Temple UP, 1997.
Clitandre, Nadege. "Diaspora of Home, Terror and Despair in the Writings of Edwidge Danticat." *Violence and Transgression in World Minority Literatures*. Ed. Rüdiger Ahrens, Franzisco Lomeli et.al. Heidelberg: Universitätsverlag Winter, 2005. 225-249.
Danticat, Edwidge. *Breath, Eyes, Memory*. New York: Soho Press.1994
Deleuze, Gilles and Felix Guattari. *Rhizom*. Berlin: Merve, 1977.
De Toro, Alfonso. "Jenseits von Postmoderne und Postkolonialität: Materialien zu einem Modell der Hybridität und des Körpers als transrelationalem, transversalem und transmedialem Wissenschaftskonzept." *Räume der Hybridität: Postkoloniale Konzepte in Theorie und Literatur*. Ed.Christof Hamann. Hildesheim: Olms, 2002. 15-52.
Di Prete, Laura. *Foreign Bodies. Trauma, Corporeality, and Textuality in Contemporary American Culture*. New York: Routledge, 2006.
Díaz, Junot. *Drown*. New York: Riverhead Books, 1996.
Donnell, Alison. *Twentieth-Century Caribbean Literature*. London: Routledge, 2006.

---

5 In this context see Henke's definition of narrative recovery: "The term *narrative recovery*, now fairly current in the field of narratology, pivots on a double *entendre* meant to evoke both the recovery of past experience through narrative articulation and the psychological reintegration of a traumatically shattered subject" (xxii).

Ferrari, Guillermina de. *Vulnerable States. Bodies of Memory in Contemporary Caribbean Fiction*. Charlottesville: U of Virginia P, 2007.
Foucault, Michel. "Film and Popular Memory." *Foucault Live*. New York: Semiotext, 1989.
Francis, Donette A. "'Silences Too Horrific to Disturb': Writing Sexual Histories in Edwidge Danticat's Breath, Eyes, Memory." *Research in African Literatures* 35:2 (Summer 2004): 75-90.
Glissant, Edouard. *Poetics of Relation*. Trans. Betsy Wing. U of Michigan P, 1997.
Goldman, Dara. *Out of Bounds. Islands and the Demarcation of Identity in the Hispanic Caribbean*. Lewisburg: Bucknell UP, 2008.
Granofsky, Ronald. *The Trauma Novel. Contemporary Symbolic Depictions of Collective Disaster*. New York: Peter Lang, 1995.
Henke, Suzette. *Shattered Subjects*. New York: St. Martin's P, 1998.
Herman, Judith Lewis. *Trauma and Recovery*. New York: Basic, 1992.
Horvitz, Deborah M. *Literary Trauma*. Albany: State U of New York P, 2000.
Kincaid, Jamaica. *Lucy*. New York: Farrar, Straus and Giroux, 1990.
Lahens, Yanik. "Anchorage and Exile. Between Writing and Place." Haiti: The Literature and Culture. *Special Issues Callaloo* 15.3. (1992): 735-46.
Lionnet, Francoise. "Inscriptions of Exile. The Body's Knowledge and the Myth of Authenticity." *Callaloo* 15.1. (1992): 30-40.
Mahlis, Kristen. "Gender and Exile. Jamaica Kincaid's Lucy." *Modern Fiction Studies* 44 (Spring 1998): 164-82.
Mardorossian, Carine. "Creolization and the Black Atlantic: Differentiated Aesthetics in Julia Alvarez's *Yo!* and Edwidge Danticat's *Breath, Eyes, Memory*." *Reclaiming Difference*. Charlottesville: U of Virginia P, 2005.114-141.
Nesbitt, Nick. *Voicing Memory: History and Subjectivity in French Caribbean Literature*. Charlottesville: U of Virginia P, 2003.
Scott, Helen. "Ou libéré? History, Transformation and the Struggle for Freedom in Edwidge Danticat's Breath, Eyes, Memory." *Haiti: Ecrire en pays/Writing under Siege*. Ed. Marie-Agnes Sourieau. Amsterdam: Rodopi, 2004. 459-478.
Suárez, Lucía. *The Tears of Hispaniola. Haitian and Dominican Diaspora Memory*. Gainesville: UP of Florida, 2006.
Tal, Kali. *Worlds of Hurt. Reading the Literatures of Trauma*. Cambridge: Cambridge UP, 1996.
Vickroy, Laura. *Trauma and Survival in Contemporary Fiction*. Charlottesville: U of Virginia P, 2002.

NARRATIVES OF ILLNESS – ILLNESS NARRATIVES

JOHN CARLOS ROWE

Disease, Culture, and Transnationalism in the Americas

Charles Mann in *1491* and Jared Diamond in *Guns, Germs, and Steel* have argued that the pre-Columbian population of the Americas was much larger than previously believed. Relying on new information provided by biological archaeologists, Mann and Diamond conclude that diseases like smallpox and influenza destroyed nearly ninety percent of pre-Columbian indigenous populations, spreading contagion even *before* the systematic contact initiated by such conquerors as Columbus, Cortès, and Pizarro.[1] Although scholars in the humanities and social sciences have long recognized the fact of European disease as a consequence of imperialism in the Americas and Canada, few of us have assessed the cultural and environmental effects of disease. New scholarship focusing on the intersection of medicine and social relations encourages us to consider the cultural consequences of illness, disease, addiction, and other medical phenomena.[2]

The question of intention is one of the major issues, which needs to be both theorized and historicized before we can proceed with much-needed research into the cultural and environmental impacts of communicable diseases. During the French and Indian War (1754-1763), British General Sir Jeffrey Amherst infamously urged Colonel Henry Bouquet "to figure some way of infecting France's Indian allies with smallpox," and on "July 13, the colonel wrote that he would attempt seeding some blankets with *Variola*, then send them to the warring tribes" (Robertson 124). R. G. Robertson notes, however, that the "intentional infection of Indians was the exception, not the norm," in part because Europeans knew too little about such contagious diseases as smallpox to use them as part of biological warfare (Robertson 124). Colonel Bouquet himself agreed to Lord Amherst's suggestion, but "expressed the hope that he would not catch the sickness himself" (Robertson 124).

---

1   Charles Mann contends that European fishermen had establishing fishing camps and traded with indigenous peoples along the northeast coast of North America for at least fifty years prior to the arrival of Columbus in 1492. Small-pox and influenza, among other contagious diseases, caused native populations to die and their survivors to move away from the coastal regions (Mann 33-68).
2   Angela Garcia discusses how heroin addiction among Hispanos in the Chimayo area of New Mexico has led to new kinship relations. Although her scholarship does not focus on culture, there are several interesting instances of cultural impact in her study, including the controversy surrounding efforts to build a memorial in the city of Chimayo dedicated to the many *veteranos*—veterans of heroin addiction—next to the Vietnam Veterans Memorial on the town Plaza (107-8).

The fact that few Europeans consciously chose to wage biological warfare does not lead inevitably to the conclusion that communicable diseases were *unintended* consequences of imperialism. Robertson claims that the "mind-set of colonial America was to quarantine smallpox, not pass it to the Indians, who could spread it to their white neighbors" (124), but his study of the smallpox epidemic of 1837-1838 at trading posts and among native peoples living along the Upper Missouri and Yellowstone rivers traces the first outbreak to an African-American crew member on the *St. Peter's*, a steamboat owned by the commercial house of Pratte and Chouteau (17). Commanded by Captain Bernard Pratte Jr., the *St. Peter's* was transporting trade goods to posts along the river at a time when the company was in dire competition with other commercial enterprises trading in the area. As a part owner of Pratte and Chouteau, Captain Pratte was very motivated to deliver the company's trade goods to Forts Clark, Union, and McKenzie and probably for this reason disregarded others' appeals that he put his sick deckhand ashore, where he could be properly cared for in full quarantine (Robertson 62). William Fulkerson, the Indian agent traveling on the *St. Peter's*, made several appeals to Captain Pratte to recognize the danger of a smallpox epidemic, but Pratte insisted that the high fever suffered by the deckhand could just as easily be ague, chickenpox, or scarlet fever as smallpox (62-63). Given the scarcity of medical doctors on the frontier, such illnesses were often diagnosed incorrectly by people without medical knowledge. As Robertson points out in the rest of his study, the consequences were disastrous for the Hidatsas, Arikaras, and Mandans living in close proximity to Forts Clark, Union, and McKenzie, as well as for several Euroamerican passengers on the steamboat and residents of nearby trading posts. The subsequent smallpox epidemic of 1837-1838 on the upper Missouri and Yellowstone rivers was one of the most deadly epidemics of the nineteenth century, reducing the Mandans in the region from as many as 2,000 to less than 150.

What were Captain Pratte's motives in refusing to recognize his crew members' illness as smallpox until it was too late? I have already suggested that the Captain's economic motives were uppermost. Needing able-bodied crew members to make the long and dangerous trip in a timely manner, he hoped that his sick deck hand might recover quickly and rejoin the rest of the crew. In fact, this is precisely what Captain Pratte ordered as soon as the African-American sailor had recovered sufficiently to work, but this decision helped infect many others on board. Just how "intentional," then, were Captain Pratte's several decisions with regard to his deckhand that resulted in the spread of smallpox on board the steamboat and then beyond its confines? Today, we might speculate reasonably that Captain Pratte's relative disregard for the African-American deckhand had at least something to do with antebellum racism and the popular perception among white Euroamericans that African Americans were more dispensable, physically more resilient, and less deserving of costly medical supplies and care. Euroamericans behaved in a similarly racist manner toward native peoples, whose exposure to communicable diseases had as much to do with Euroamericans' carelessness and disregard of other cultural, biological, and environmental factors as with their ignorance of the diseases they carried. Reframing the question of "intention" in terms of "responsibility," rather than intentional agency, might help us understand better the extent to which Europeans should (or should not) be held accountable for the spread of infectious diseases and the subsequent genocide they caused in the Americas and Canada.

Consider the more tenuous case for the intentional spread of communicable diseases posed by Hernando De Soto's passage through the Southeast of North America between 1539 and 1543. Traveling with a "private army" of 600 men, transported by 200 horses, and supplied in part by 300 pigs, De Soto "wandered through what are now Florida, Georgia, North and South Carolina, Tennessee, Alabama, Mississippi, Arkansas, Texas, and Louisiana, looking for gold and wrecking most everything [he] touched" (Mann 107). Although he died of fever at the end of his expedition, which had realized little beyond the destruction it left in its path, De Soto was fearless in his encounters with native peoples, brazenly marching into the numerous cities he encountered, demanding food, and marching out again (Mann 108). Between what is now Florida and Arkansas, De Soto's expedition encountered densely populated regions, fierce native resistance, and country "thickly set with great towns […]" (as quoted in Mann 108). Europeans did not visit the Mississippi Valley again until early 1682, when La Salle "passed through the area where De Soto had found cities cheek by jowl," only to discover the region "deserted," without encountering an Indian village "for two hundred miles" (108).

The conclusion drawn by the anthropologist Charles Hudson is that De Soto's pigs had spread measles, influenza, and smallpox that attacked native peoples with such virulence that the densely populated Mississippi Valley was emptied before La Salle's arrival a century and a half later (Mann 107-108). Mann analyzes the spread of infectious diseases by the domesticated animals accompanying the *Conquistadores* to explain how native cultures vanished so quickly and native resistance so often evaporated as indigenous armies were stricken with epidemics. One powerful explanation for why Hérnan Cortés's return to Tenochtitlan was successful, despite the Aztecs' resounding defeat and expulsion of his small army in their first engagement, was that the capital had been swept by a smallpox epidemic just after Cortés's first retreat (Mann 141-143).

Were these conquerors (and others, like Pizarro) just lucky, enlisting unwittingly the different immune systems and DNA of native peoples? Smallpox, or *Variola major* had swept through medieval Europe every "five or ten years," killing many but also immunizing those who survived and providing their children with "an increased resistance—but not immunity—to the illness"

(Robertson 43). Although "acquired immunity," generally simulated by exposure to smallpox scabs or pus, had been "used in India for over 1,000 years and in China since the Sung Dynasty (AD 960-1279)," European inoculations with smallpox were not attempted until 1700 and well into the late eighteenth century such practices were considered experimental (Robertson 46-47). It is also worth noting that most people choosing inoculation tended to belong to the upper classes and thus had the benefits of medical advice, up-to-date scientific information, and the economic means to afford inoculation. The "complete inoculation process required between one and two months to complete. Inoculees spent the first half of the time resting and improving their diet if they had a competent inoculator; or bleeding, vomiting, and starving if they did not. During the second half of the procedures, the inoculees were bedridden with small pox" (Robertson 50).

In the epidemic of 1837-1838, partial efforts were made to vaccinate Euroamericans and some native peoples against smallpox, but reliable medical supplies were not provided in sufficient quantities to prevent an epidemic. Just five years earlier, the twenty-second Congress on May 5, 1832 "approved $ 12,000" to vaccinate "all the nation's Indians," directing the Secretary of War to carry out the operation (Robertson 224). But these "good intentions fell prey to bureaucratic indifference and, perhaps, wanton prejudice" (224-225). Successful vaccination on the frontier was a difficult task, given the susceptibility of the vaccines to damage by heat, water, and other contaminants and that they be administered by qualified physicians, few of whom were willing to travel to remote regions to work with potentially hostile patients. Tangled up with these frontier contingencies are the open prejudices of Euroamericans, many of whom considered withholding vaccination would serve the larger purpose of "solving" the "Indian problem." Robertson notes that on May 9, 1832, Secretary of War Lewis Cass "wrote John Dougherty, the senior Indian agent for the upper Missouri, that he should not vaccinate any tribes above the [territory occupied by] the Arikaras" (Robertson 225). One conclusion might be that Cass did not believe his limited financial resources could pay for vaccines and doctors to serve that remote territory; another conclusion is that Cass was punishing hostile Blackfeet, who "regularly harassed American trapping brigades" in the region (225). Indeed, the Blackfeet were devastated by repeated smallpox epidemics between the 1830s and 1880s (Welch 30-37). In short, the boundaries separating conscious intentions, hidden agendas, mere carelessness, ignorance, and unavoidable accident are difficult to draw.

Walter Mignolo has argued that Spanish imperialism depended crucially on the affirmation of European civilization by rendering native cultures in the Western Hemisphere as primitive and uncivilized. In *The Darker Side of the Renaissance*, he argues that European scholars largely supported the religious efforts of missionaries to convert "pagan Indians" by asserting not only the authority of the Bible but also the long traditions of print-based culture on which

European civilization was built. The Spanish burnt an enormous amount of the indigenous archive they encountered in the Western Hemisphere. Sometimes this destruction was a consequence of military strategy, as when Cortés set fire to Tenochtitlan to cover his retreat, but more often it was a deliberate effort to destroy "pagan" and "diabolical" texts. Mignolo devotes considerable attention to the "colonial semiosis" that included not only massive encyclopedic efforts in sixteenth and seventeenth-century Europe, such as Bernardino Sahagún's *Florentine Codex* (1578) and Francis Bacon's *Novum Organum* (1620) (200-202), and systematic efforts to deny the cultural legitimacy of such semiotic systems as the Incan Quipu and Mexica Amoxtli, Huehuetlatolli, and Toltecáyotl, to mention only the most prominent genres of hieroglyphic and oral-formulaic representation used by indigenous peoples in the Western Hemisphere (Mignolo 125-216).

For Mignolo, modern imperialism works in large part by dismantling the civilization of the conquered and rendering them subaltern as a consequence of their growing dependence on the imperial power's epistemology. In nineteenth-century North America, U.S. relations with native peoples are generally characterized by a disparity between Euroamerican "civilization" and native "primitivism" that has long been considered fundamental to the Myth of the Vanishing American. When De Soto and his private army forced their way into native cities in the Southeast to demand food, they represented graphically the various ways Euroamericans ignored cultural differences and assumed their own superiority. Lewis Cass's decision to withhold vaccine from the Blackfeet may be subtler, but it also displays his indifference, if not hostility, to the social integrity of the Blackfeet Nation.

What Mignolo terms Spanish imperialism's "denial of coevalness," which means the systematic refusal to acknowledge a foreign culture's potential equality with your own, is reinforced by communicable diseases that affected native peoples in greater numbers and more fatalities than Europeans. Like Todorov's much disputed argument in *The Conquest of America* that the sophistication of European semiotics assisted the Spanish and Portuguese in conquering native peoples, so the history of communicable disease appears to favor the survival of Europeans over "Indians" and thus lead to the conclusion that European culture and peoples are somehow "superior." Jared Diamond's thesis is that the domestication of animals in Europe, a practice acquired originally from the Middle East, exposed Europeans to communicable diseases, such as smallpox, measles, and influenza, early enough historically to enable surviving Europeans to develop immunities in sufficient numbers for their populations to grow, even though they faced repeated epidemics from the Middle Ages through the nineteenth century.

Evolutionary biologists have argued that the relative success of Europeans in surviving epidemics and pandemics has much to do with their genetic diversity. Because the original newcomers to the Western Hemisphere were probably small in number, "their gene pool was correspondingly restricted, which meant that Indian biochemistry was and is unusually homogeneous" (Mann 114). Neither genetic diversity nor homogeneity is preferable (or "superior") in strictly evolutionary terms. Although genetic diversity protected Europeans from total or *de facto* extinction by communicable diseases, genetic homogeneity in the Western Hemisphere protected native peoples from diseases caused by "deleterious genes" more likely to be found in genetically diverse circumstances. Thus before European contact, American Indians were "free or almost free of cystic fibrosis, Huntington's chorea, newborn anemia, asthma, and (possibly) juvenile diabetes" (Mann 114).

The problems begin when genetically diverse peoples come into contact with genetically homogeneous peoples. Genetic homogeneity means that such communities are affected much more broadly by communicable diseases like smallpox, influenza, measles, and chicken pox. In the Western Hemisphere, contact with Europeans carrying these diseases and pathogens resulted in widespread death in genetically homogeneous Amerindian communities, in many cases extinguishing them. What, in fact, do we mean by "extinction"? Of course, we understand the meaning of the extinction of a specific species, such as the Dodo bird or Passenger Pigeon. But extinction of human groups involves the loss of their abilities to maintain the basic economic, social, and cultural practices that give such groups distinctive identities. Native American survivors of the smallpox epidemic of 1837-1838, for example, moved in with different tribes, gradually adapting to their host tribe's practices, if they did not carry the disease to their hosts. Throughout the Western Hemisphere, large and small communities reduced by disease, warfare with each other and with Europeans, and ecological factors often directly related to these new socioeconomic conditions reached points of disfunctionality and were either subject to conquest or diaspora.

Thus both the imperialist claim to a "superior civilization" as the justification for the colonization of nominally more "primitive" peoples *and* the complementary claim to biological superiority must be challenged, if we acknowledge that in colonial encounters of Amerindians and Europeans there were simply semiotic and biological differences without inherently "positive" or "negative" terms. Traditional disciplinary distinctions between cultural studies and biological sciences suggest that diseases and cultural destruction operated in separate social registers, complementing each other to be sure in the work of imperial Conquest but hardly intersecting as "techniques" of imperialist control. Yet there are several ways in which we might dispute this notion of a "separate spheres," in which biological and cultural destruction collaborate and thus must be studied together. To be sure, archaeological biology is an emergent field in which such work is already being done, but I want to extend its insights to the more familiar humanistic areas in which I have been trained.

In the nineteenth century, Euroamerican sympathies for the plight of the Native American were integral to the perceived superiority of Europeans over indigenous peoples and their presumed "primitivism." We know, of course, that Euroamerican visual, plastic, theatrical, and verbal arts played major parts in legitimating the Myth of the Noble Savage, but artistic production often contributed directly to the spread of communicable diseases and thus the genocidal work of imperialism. When George Catlin visited the Upper Missouri in 1832, he "bragged about the healthfulness of the country and declared it immune to disease," confirming verbally the physical strength, health, and beauty of the Native American subjects of his portraits (Dippie 329). Only five years later, the epidemic of 1837-1838 would reduce the Mandans he visited in the region from "preepidemic population estimates [...] from 1,500 to 2,000" to the "postepidemic" 150 or less (Dippie 329). When Catlin addressed a Boston audience in 1838, "he left his listeners with the firm impression that the tribe was 'now extinct'" (Dippie 329). Catlin was one of the few Euroamerican travelers in the West to express indignation regarding the spread of communicable diseases to native peoples, complaining in *Letters and Notes* that the presumed "inevitability" of the Indian's extinction "was not inevitable," laying the blame squarely on "'the system of trade, and the small-pox' that 'have been the great and wholesale destroyers of these poor people'" (Trachtenberg 16). Despite his sympathy with native Americans' suffering, Catlin was not above capitalizing on their "disappearance," which would mean "that his pictorial record could never be duplicated, an incredible stroke of good fortune from the standpoint of self-interest, which alone might account for [his father] Putnam Catlin's callous comment that the 'shocking calamity' that had befallen the Mandans would 'greatly increase the value' of his son's gallery" (Dippie 329-330).[3]

When Catlin toured Europe in the early 1840s with a party of Canadian Ojibwas, illustrated in his *Notes of Eight Years' Travel and Residence in Europe* (1848), the party of eleven "was increased by one birth and reduced by" a total of seven deaths from smallpox by the end of their tour (Dippie 109). Just as the more famous Pocahontas (c. 1595-1617) had died probably of smallpox at Gravesend while preparing to return from England to Virginia, so these exhibited Indians had suffered the costs of travel to the metropolitan centers of imperial power. Admitting that the exhibition of these Ojibwas had done nothing to advance their political causes, tacitly understanding he had exploited their exoticism to boost his own aesthetic reputation and the value of his paintings of Native American life, Catlin recognized the ideological contradictions of his conduct and art (Dippie 109). Like some perverse version of Edgar Allan Poe's famous story "The Oval Portrait" (1845), Pocahontas and Catlin's Ojib-

---

3   Catlin's aim was to sell his gallery of Native American portraits to the Smithsonian, an institution founded in part to "preserve" the cultural artifacts of what its curators considered the rapidly vanishing Native American way of life.

was are "memorialized" in literary and pictorial forms of Western art in direct proportion to the mortal risks they took as unwilling travelers.

I have said little thus far about the consequences of epidemic diseases for the environment, but the spread of foreign diseases can in itself be considered a form of "pollution" with comparable environmental impacts. North American Indians, despite their tribal differences, shared the common belief in the wholeness of the natural world and how their minds and bodies figured into such an ecology. In practical terms, of course, hunting-gathering societies often starve when a significant percentage of their hunters and gatherers are sick, as is the case with epidemic diseases like smallpox. Charles Mann writes about the crucial roles indigenous peoples played in maintaining their natural resources from selective hunting of game to strategic firing of grass and forest lands to maintain healthy prairies and woodlands. Imperial encroachments on native peoples' territories certainly contributed to changes in the natural environment in the Americas, but these conventional political actions should be considered in conjunction with the effects of disease. As tribal people were forced onto reservations in the post-Civil War period, they also became increasingly dependent on government food supplies and Euroamerican farming practices. The U.S. government either at the federal level or as represented by the reservation's Indian agent commonly distributed fewer supplies and materials to Indians than had actually been allocated. Indeed, the unevenness of governmental support for Native Americans matched the eccentric distribution of medicine and medical care. Native people "starved" on the reservations, and famine is another form of communicable "illness," which certainly did reach epidemic proportions on many reservations.

Myths of the superiority of Western Civilization have certainly been reinforced by the apparently superstitious responses of indigenous peoples to communicable diseases. To be sure, many of the treatments performed by indigenous medicine men and shamans demonstrated ignorance of the etiology and spread of diseases like smallpox and influenza, but Europeans knew nothing about the treatment of smallpox or influenza during seventeenth-century contact and the medical developments of the late eighteenth and nineteenth century in treating such diseases were new to Western medicine and only partially effective. Indigenous peoples in regular contact with Euroamericans did learn the benefits of inoculation against smallpox and appealed for it in many cases, but it is equally striking how many native accounts represent disease as part of the broader environmental damage committed by the European conquerors. As late as Sarah Winnemucca's *Life among the Paiutes* (1883), she recalls how the spread of smallpox among the Northern Paiutes was understood by members of her tribe as "poison" spread by the whites in the Truckee River. Many other indigenous cultural responses to communicable diseases link these biological hazards with the Euroamerican destruction of the buffalo herds and other foods sources, the outright murder of indigenous peoples occupying lands desired by westward moving settlers, and other violations of the nature-culture bond so important for indigenous peoples.

In the epidemic of 1837-1838 in the upper Missouri and Yellowstone rivers, Mah-to-toh-pa (Four Bears), a Mandan War Chief, was reputed to have said the following on July 30, 1837, the day he died of smallpox:

> My Friends one and all, Listen to what I have to say—Ever since I can remember, I have loved the Whites, [...] I have never wronged a White Man, [...] I was always ready to die for them, [...] and how have they repaid it! With ingratitude! [...] I have been in Many Battles, and often Wounded, but the Wounds of My enemies I exhalt [sic] in, but to day I am Wounded, and by Whom, by those same White Dogs that I have always Considered, and treated as Brothers. I do not fear Death my friends. You Know it, but to die with my face rotten, that even the Wolves will shrink with horror at seeing Me, [...] Think of your Wives, Children, Brothers, Sisters, Friends, and in fact all that you hold dear, are all Dead, or Dying, with their faces all rotten, caused by those dogs the whites, think of all that My friends, and rise all together and Not leave one of them alive. (qtd. in Robertson xvii)

Four Bears' call for revolt against the Europeans who had brought the smallpox to the Fort Clark area was not an isolated event. Mandan warriors mourning family members threatened the *bourgeois* of Fort Clark on numerous occasions during the epidemic, believing with other area tribes that "the whites had employed some sorcery to attack" native peoples (Robertson 170). The Assiniboines "vowed to set fire to Fort Union and kill every trader," and Chief Le Vieux Gauche (Old Left Hand) burnt "his American flag" in protest of the smallpox epidemic brought by Euroamericans and organized his dwindling warriors for an assault on the fort (Robertson 206).

The general accusation of "white sorcery" made by different tribes decimated in the 1837-1838 epidemic was consistent with the medical treatment most tribes followed. Generally, tribal shamans brought family members into close proximity with the afflicted, chanting to drive out the evil spirits, and of course thereby spread the disease to those family members, themselves, and the next patient treated. Quarantine of smallpox patients was generally not practiced in Native American communities. The Native American interpretation of smallpox and other communicable diseases as Euroamerican sorcery certainly contributed to their outright hostility, although in many cases such epidemics made military resistance impractical or ineffective. The Plains Wars of the post-Civil War era are usually attributed to Native American anger regarding broken treaties, displacement of the Bison by frontier immigrants, and routine massacres of native peoples (especially women, children, and the elderly) by the U.S. Army and local militias intent on "controlling" so-called "renegades." Such explanations seem motivated primarily by Euroamerican values regarding disputes over property, resources, and deliberate violence. But the long history of epidemics was also a motivation for Native American armed resistance.

In his classic study *The Ghost-Dance Religion and the Sioux Outbreak of 1890* (1896), James Mooney considered the Ghost-Dance Religion to be an unwitting enactment of Native American apocalypse. Wovoka tells Mooney that he received his "vision" when he "was stricken down by a severe fever" and that "while he was still sick there occurred an eclipse of the sun," which Mooney notes "always excites a great alarm among primitive peoples," then quoting Wovoka that "'when the sun died,' [...] he went to sleep in the daytime and was taken up to heaven" (Mooney 773). Michael Elliott concludes that Mooney's account of Wovoka's vision attributes the prophet's spiritual experience to the coincidence of his personal illness and a solar eclipse (Elliott 112). Just as Western ethnographers interpret Lakota "vision quests" as dependent on the fasting, lack of sleep, and other physical hardships of the young warriors, so Mooney wants Wovoka's epiphany to be the result of material circumstances. Generalizing his personal experience to that of all native peoples, Wovoka creates an appealing illusion that testifies to the inability of native people to overcome their premodern conditions and thus their inabilities to adapt to the modern, secular world.

Another interpretation of the Ghost-Dance Religion is that Wovoka's "severe fever" is symbolic of the communicable diseases that have ravaged native peoples since the arrival of the Europeans. Such illnesses did in fact cause many to experience the death of the sun, whether this means literal death or the diminution of the sun's natural divinity and power.[4] As symbolic actions, Wovoka's and nature's "illnesses" may also suggest sacrificial transumption, analogous to Christ's crucifixion, which is ritualized in the performance of the "Ghost Dance."[5] The Performance of the Ghost Dance empowers those who do the dance properly and those who identify with the dancers (either as audience or as followers of the religion) as some sort of "immunization" against white "sorcery." In this speculative and undeveloped reading, the aesthetic and communal functions of the Ghost Dance "restore" the health of the people, which means either the literal or symbolic return of the bison—the means of sustaining life—and the literal or symbolic return of the ancestors—the cultural heritage of the tribes following the religion. Insofar as the Ghost-Dance Religion was received by Native Americans as a pan-Indian, trans-tribal movement, ex-

---

4   In Lakota cultures, for example, Wakan-tanka is the unifying force of nature and often represented by the sun.
5   Mooney contends that Wovoka denied any claim "to be Christ, the Son of God, as so often has been asserted in print" (773), but the Ghost-Dance Religion obviously adapts many elements of Christianity, including the general idea of sacrifice, transumption, and resurrection. Wovoka's denial that he emulated Christ is not surprising, both in the context of Mooney's "scientific" account and Wovoka's awareness that Euroamericans would consider any Indian "imitatio Christi" to be blasphemous. Elliott notes that Mooney concluded that Wovoka was "something of an assimilationist," supporting the usual idea that the Ghost-Dance Religion hybridizes Christian and Paiute *figurae* (Elliott 110).

tending from the Great Basin of the Northern Paiutes to Blackfeet, Piegan, and Shoshone in the Rocky Mountains to Cheyenne, and Lakota Sioux of the Great Plains, then the "revival" and restored "health" it represents can be understood as symbolic of such cooperation and consolidation of forces.

Even the controversial "ghost shirt," which was "a garment some Sioux wore in the belief that it would stop bullets," but which Wovoka told Mooney he "disclaimed all responsibility for," could be interpreted as following the internal logic of the Ghost-Dance Religion's *healing* powers (Mooney 772-773). In 1889, when the Oglala Sioux Nick Black Elk returned to the Pine Ridge Reservation after touring with Buffalo Bill Cody's Wild West Show, he was quickly attracted to Wovoka and the Ghost-Dance Religion and its pan-Indian promise: "Word came to us that the Indians were beginning to dance everywhere" (*BE* 249). He recounts how he made several Ghost Shirts prior to performing in his first Ghost Dance, experiencing his own spiritual vision, and subsequently riding into battle at Wounded Knee wearing one that by his account *does* protect him from harm (*BE* 243). Black Elk was both a medicine man and a holy man in his career, the latter position usually requiring apprenticeship as a healer in Lakota society. Was the "ghost shirt" simply a superstition adopted by Lakota (and some other Plains' Indians) desperate for protection against what Black Elk elsewhere describes as the "flood" of "wasichus" (white people), including the epidemics, murders, and theft that inevitably trailed along with them? Or is the "ghost shirt" suggestive of comprehensive, even coordinated, cultural means native peoples used to resist the "white sorcery" they encountered in such acts of imperial violence?

The answer to this rhetorical question is by no means simple or easy, because it will involve much more detailed investigations into the cultural practices and spiritual activities of different native peoples in the many different historical stages of European contact. My examples are tribally and historically scattered, even incoherent, but they are intended to point us toward interpretations of indigenous cultural and religious media that will acknowledge first the *reality* of disease for native peoples and second their identification of many such diseases with the threats posed to their survival by Euroamericans. We now know that many pre-Columbian medical procedures in the Western Hemisphere, including surgeries and the use of herbal medicines, were very successful in the treatment of illnesses known to native peoples. The problems confronting Native Americans with diseases like smallpox, measles, and influenza included their novelty, the unevenness (in many cases deliberately so) of medical treatment and the distribution of medicines by Euroamericans to native peoples, and the integration of disease with other imperial practices of genocide, whether intentionally (as in Lord Amherst's notorious case) or by the sort of perverse serendipity that must have reinforced native Americans' perceptions of imperial conquest as "white sorcery," whether it was conducted by military assault or biological warfare.

In *Killing Custer* (1994), James Welch recounts the Marias River Massacre (Baker Massacre) of January 22, 1870, when Colonel E. M. Baker launched an attack on a peaceful Blackfoot village, its members bundled up against winter cold of twenty degrees below zero and most villagers suffering from an outbreak of the "white scabs" (smallpox). Killing 173 men, women, and children, then setting the village of about forty tepees ablaze, Baker was aware that he was attacking the wrong village (Welch 30-31). Welch concludes his novel, *Fools Crow* (1986), with a fictional account of the historical massacre, using the event to mark the end of resistance by the Blackfeet Nation. As he writes in *Killing Custer*, the Blackfeet "never raised arms against the United States again" (Welch 37). Why, Welch wonders, has such an injustice against native peoples been forgotten while George Armstrong Custer's defeat at the Little Big Horn only six years later has been so relentlessly monumentalized (Welch 46)?[6]

Welch's entire career as a Blackfeet writer is itself a Native American cultural response to the migratory power of communicable diseases brought by Europeans to the Western Hemisphere. "Throughout the contact period with the whites, smallpox epidemics raged periodically, almost systematically," Welch writes, adding an interesting cultural complement: "In 1837, three years after Prince Maximilian, the German naturalist and explorer, and the Swiss artist Karl Bodmer visited a Mandan village on the upper Missouri and remarked on the Indians' fine appearance, the tribe had been reduced from sixteen hundred to only one hundred" (Welch 34). Maximilian and Bodmer visited in 1834 one of those Mandan villages that would be devastated in the 1837-1838 epidemic on the Upper Missouri and Yellowstone rivers discussed earlier in this paper. Like Du Bois rhetorical question in *Darkwater* (1920) whether or not the glories of European culture were worth the human costs of the slave trade on which that culture depended, Welch suggests that the Prince's enlightened natural science and the Swiss artist's exquisite paintings of the West must be weighed against the human cost of those migrations that first brought Europeans to the Western Hemisphere (Rowe 208). In his effort to represent Blackfeet people at various stages of their historical contact with Euroamericans, Welch contributes his own versions of indigenous representation as means of countering the political and aesthetic "cover-ups" of Western representations of Native Americans.

---

6   The Marias River Massacre was only one among many such massacres by the U.S. Army and local militias during the Plains Wars and other conflicts during westward expansion, but historians generally ignore the murder of native people when calculating the "worst" massacres in U.S. history. The Mountain Meadows Massacre of September 11, 1857, in which Mormons disguised as Paiute and Ute Indians, attacked the Fancher wagon train, killing 120 Arkansas emigrants to California, is generally treated as the "worst massacre in U.S. history" prior to 9/11. See Sally Denton, *American Massacre* (2003).

What cultural and human production, what *lives*, might have resulted from those sixteen hundred souls inhabiting what is now northern Montana had that single Mandan village not been reduced to "only one hundred"? What difference would it have made had 100 million inhabitants of the Western Hemisphere maintained that demographic or, more likely, have grown to even more than one-third of the world's population between 1492 and 1650? Would the social, economic, political, ethnic, and biomedical diversity of such a critical mass of Amerindians have responded differently to European imperialism than what is so often represented in the Myth of the Vanishing American and its complements, the Ghost-Dance Religion and the Peruvian Myth of the Inca Rey?[7] Whether communicable diseases brought by the Europeans affect Amerindian cultures as a consequence of reducing the numbers of people needed for a society to produce, transmit, and preserve "culture" or the effects of such diseases are registered in far more complex ways within cultural works that cross specific tribal, territorial, and generic boundaries, epidemic and pandemic diseases are integral aspects of migrations and diasporas. The spread of such diseases and their medical treatment have enduring biomedical, social, economic, political, cultural, psychological, environmental, and ethical consequences we must study and understand as integral to postcolonial and cultural studies of the Western Hemisphere.

Works Cited

Denton, Sally. *American Massacre: The Tragedy at Mountain Meadows, September 11, 1857*. New York: Alfred A. Knopf, 2003.

Diamond, Jared. *Guns, Germs, and Steel: The Fates of Human Societies*. New York: W. W. Norton, 1997.

Dippie, Brian W. *Catlin and His Contemporaries: The Politics of Patronage*. Lincoln: University of Nebraska Press, 1990.

Elliott, Michael A. *The Culture Concept: Writing and Difference in the Age of Realism*. Minneapolis: University of Minnesota Press, 2002.

Garcia, Angela. *The Pastoral Clinic: Addiction and Dispossession along the Rio Grande*. Berkeley: University of California Press, 2010.

---

7   The myth of the Inca Rey dates from early eighteenth-century Peru, when legends circulated that a disembodied head of an Incan King would rise above the Andes to announce the return of Incan royal authority, expulsion of the Spanish imperial powers, and the resurrection of those murdered by European imperialists. I have often thought that the severed head of the revolutionary Babo, displayed in the central square of Lima, at the end of Herman Melville's *Benito Cereno* (1855) draws on this Amerindian legend, even though Babo himself is, of course, from Senegal.

Mann, Charles C. *1491: New Revelations of the Americas before Columbus*. New York: Random House, Inc., 2006.

Mignolo, Walter. *The Darker Side of the Renaissance: Literacy, Territoriality, and Colonization*. University of Michigan Press, 1995.

Mooney, James. *The Ghost-Dance Religion and the Sioux Outbreak of 1890*. 1896: Rpt. Lincoln: University of Nebraska Press, 1991.

Neihardt, John G. *Black Elk Speaks: Being the Life Story of a Holy Man of the Oglala Sioux*. Lincoln: University of Nebraska Press, 1961.

Robertson, R. G. *Rotting Face: Smallpox and the American Indian*. Caldwell, Idaho: Caxton Press, 2001.

Rowe, John Carlos. *Literary Culture and U.S. Imperialism: From the Revolution to World War II*. New York: Oxford University Press, 2000.

Trachtenberg, Alan. *Staging Indians, Making Americans, 1880-1930*. New York: Hill and Wang, 2004.

Welch, James. *Fools Crow*. New York: Viking, 1986.

Welch, James with Paul Stekler. *Killing Custer: The Battle of the Little Bighorn and the Fate of the Plains Indians*. New York: Penguin Books, 1995.

MARC PRIEWE

Making Sense of Morbidity in Early American Autobiography

Historians have repeatedly claimed the seventeenth century as an era of transition from experience to science and, with regard to the explorative and explanatory dominance over the human body, from religion to medicine.[1] In England, the shift from a mystical occult epistemology to rationalism is often seen as coinciding with the Restoration and the founding of the Royal Society of London in 1661. The suggested ruptural emancipation of one epistemic system from another is, however, misleading; the decline of Renaissance occultism has to be seen as a concomitant rather than a mere opposing force to the rise of the scientific revolution: Aside from its departure from occult traditions, the new sciences followed a mode of inquiry based on reason and empiricism, and, as a result, also began to discard assumptions about divine intention and intervention with regard to disease. Hence, with the emergence of medicine as a scientific field during the Renaissance, the efforts of healers to discover regularities, patterns, and functions of the body repeatedly collided with religious doctrines that saw the body as a fascinating manifestation of Providence, whose proper workings were ultimately hidden from human knowledge.[2]

In early New England, however, the competition and even hostility between religion and medical science was far less developed than in the mother country; in fact, both epistemologies and modes of practical healing coexisted and at times complemented each other, not least because economic and demographic conditions produced the personal union of minister and physician as the primary healing figure in colonial towns. Only at the outset of the eighteenth century did New England attract a rising number of secular physicians, and colonists increasingly incorporated a practical openness toward scientific discoveries in the field of medicine. At the same time, with the growing confidence in new medical inventions and achievements, the two knowledge systems slowly diverged, especially with regard to the hierarchy of authority over interpreting and treating the body adequately. The tensions between religious

---

1 For the slow and dynamic shift from occultism to science, see Webster; Vickers. For a focus on the medicine of early modern Europe, see Grell/Cunningham; French/Wear. Recent introductions to the history of medicine include: Magner; Gonzalez-Crussi.
2 This is not to argue that medicine and religion were entirely at odds with each other during the early modern period. As Charles Webster observes, "throughout the Scientific Revolution, Christian eschatology provided an undiminishing incentive towards science, if not a primary motivating factor" (48). The argument that Protestantism was generally conducive to the new sciences is further elaborated by proponents of the Merton thesis (Cohen).

and scientific doctrines were based on contested principles that represented differential medical approaches: if, for instance, certain bodily ailments constituted signs of divine punishment or tests of faith—as theologians repeatedly argued—then to what extent may or should human beings interfere in the course of illness and, by doing so, in God's will and omnipotence?

This and other questions pertaining to the personal and collective signification of disease were discussed publicly—from pulpits and in print—but were also part of private reflections recorded in Puritan spiritual autobiographies. Therein, one especially finds a symbolic encoding of illness that expresses a deep-rooted cultural linkage between morbidity and morality. According to this belief, some people "deserved" an illness due to their (sinful) behavior, while for others it marked a necessary trial or corrective measure sanctioned by the divine. Illness and infirmity were often perceived as compromising the patient's privacy because they opened the body's "narrative"—the story about the sufferer's life and conduct—to the scrutiny of colonial society. In this essay, I want to investigate how Puritan autobiographical writings by John Winthrop, Thomas Shepard, Anne Bradstreet, John Dane, and Increase Mather configure illness *as* morbidity in textual space. In all personal narratives surveyed here, disease experiences play an important role in the recognition of sin. In some cases, illness serves as a means of entering into a covenant with God and with one's community; in others, illness reveals contradictions in the confessor's spiritual estate, often causing colonists to become melancholic or even insane; in still others, medical experiences and/or discourses assume a decisively public function, reminding New England colonists that disease signals impending apocalypse.

I.

In the personal reflections, aptly named "Experiencia," of Massachusetts Bay governor John Winthrop, illness induces a crisis of the self. It marks a life-changing event that estranges the writer from his community of worldly acquaintances and introduces him to Christian fellowship with God and other believers. Yet, Winthrop, in his younger years, is unable to assess fully the contradiction between a self who is convinced of its qualification for entering into a covenant with God and the need of humiliation and instruction through illness. The future governor's first calling at age 19 is followed by a life-long wavering between assurance of salvation and lingering doubts. At several instances along the path of conversion, Winthrop is forced to consider sicknesses as occasions for reflecting his relation with the divine. In 1611, an unspecified disease causes Winthrop to realize his "bould running's out against conscience," which he then, "passed over with slight repentance" (*Winthrop Papers* I, 164). It seems as if the sick body forces Winthrop to come to terms with the shallowness, superficiality, and insincerity of his piety. During moments of intense pain and discomfort, the writer understands the presence of a superior force that shows an obvious concern for the sinner/sufferer. By voicing this observation, Winthrop echoes the theme of ambivalent contact with the divine during illness—sickness as both spiritually debasing and uplifting—that is evident in many texts produced by seventeenth-century New Englanders.

In 1628, at age thirty-nine, Winthrop interprets another sickness and recovery as indications of God's special favor. Having now passed mid-life, the frailty, limitations, and finite nature of the human body become vivid to the ill Winthrop, who admits that only few occasions in his life have brought him closer to God and have intensified his connection with the community he helped govern. In contrast to most lay conversion narratives given before New England congregations, Winthrop not only relates that illness is an abstract turning point but also depicts the manifestations of his growth in grace in relative detail. The signs of sanctification which sickness renders visible include overcoming his tobacco addiction and the communal outpouring of affection for the Bay Colony leader. However, the greatest benefit from illness, as Winthrop makes sure to iterate, was "the assurance he gave me of my salvation, and grace over some corruptions which had gotten masterye of me, which increased my experience of his trueth and faithfullnesse in disposing the worst condition of his children to their best good" (*Winthrop Papers* I, 412-413). Winthrop implicitly claims that he has passed the test of faith that God had devised by "sending" him an illness. In doing so, he establishes typological references to the Book of Job, when, instead of turning away from God, his allegiance is rewarded by divine favors, including the health of his wife and the well-being of his community.

So far, Winthrop's journal entries are fully aligned with the dominant Puritan hermeneutics of illness. In the final section of "Experiencia," however, the stability of illness signs and their underlying spiritual meanings undergo a noteworthy crisis. In the spring of 1637, Winthrop confesses to his journal his personal flirtations with Antinomianism during the previous months. The retrospective confession portrays an individual who grapples with the promise of free grace, assurance of salvation, and immediate, emotional interaction with the divine, on the one hand, and with the contradictions between his public and private personae, on the other. As Winthrop is instigating and undertaking the prosecution and banishment of Anne Hutchinson, his personal relations present a writing self on trial for deviating from the path of religious orthodoxy.[3] His initiation into Antinomianism is, similar to other Winthropean religious revelations, prompted by illness: "I came to see more clearly into the covenant of free grace. First therefore hee laid a sore affliction upon mee wherein hee laid

---

3   Winthrop took an active part in the court hearings of Anne Hutchinson during the summer of 1637. For a more detailed account of the events surrounding the Antinomian Crisis, see Winship; Stoever.

me lower in myne owne eyes then at any time before, and showed mee the emptiness of all my guifts, and parts" (*Winthrop Papers* I, 159). While the writing subject considers illness as a token of the sanctity of Antinomianism, Winthrop soon has to realize that he erred in his reading of disease. The author attributes this misreading to his own inability to discern the truth of God's message, rather than to a misguided sign by the sender. After a period of reflection, he realizes that "[t]he Doctrine of justification lately taught here, took mee in as drowsy a condition," leading him to condemn Antinomianism in private and to further prosecute it in public (*Winthrop Papers* I, 160). The emphasis on the "drowsy a condition" configures free grace theology as a momentary lapse of reason, a mental illness even, that can only be overcome by returning to "healthy" orthodoxy. Moreover, Winthrop's "as if" stagings of Antinomian conviction allow him to test his written version of self about its continual concordance with norms and values of Puritan faith.

These journal entries highlight the governor's position toward, and failing rhetorical battle against, Antinomianism during the court hearings of Newton/Cambridge in 1637. Winthrop's projection of his repressed Antinomian convictions on a culturally deviant midwife and self-styled prophet proves a hindrance during his attempted annihilation of Anne Hutchinson in court and later in narrative space. In contrast to Hutchinson, who maintained and defended her beliefs in public, Winthrop's "Experiencia" envisions privately how the trial should have proceeded: the transgressor from the path of orthodoxy and proper religious and social conviction realizes the errors of the free grace position, repents, and returns to the mainstream of New England Calvinism. As much as one may want to criticize Winthrop's self-narrative as a display of hypocrisy and moral double standard, the juxtaposition of the doubting self and the comparatively self-assured public prosecutor guided by medical providentialism affords rare insights into the complexities of an early New England psyche. While it may seem easy and convenient to diagnose the author's changing positions on Antinomianism as schizophrenic, the connection between illness and spiritual estates fosters an ambiguous and multidimensional quest for conversion that is actually in full keeping with orthodoxy. Taken as a whole, Winthrop's "Experiencia" illustrates how illness draws the self further into a landscape of interiority. The author's employment, positioning, and verbalization of pain and suffering in his fragmented life narrative ties in with some of the main Puritan usages of illness-induced analysis of the self: illness gives cause for further introspection; the bodily state of exception provides time and occasion for spiritual meditations and musings; deliverance from illness is a special providential intervention by God, difficult to read at times, but ultimately designed to lead the faithful toward grace.

II.

One of Winthrop's collaborators during the prosecution of Anne Hutchinson was Cambridge minister, Thomas Shepard. Unlike Winthrop, who failed to convict the Antinomian leader of heresy and unlawful behavior, Shepard's interrogation of the accused was more successful in unveiling the theological transgressions of the "free gracers." In Shepard's mid-seventeenth century autobiography the Hutchinson trial plays no role, contrary to Winthrop's self-narrative. What unites the autobiographies of the two early leaders of New England is that illness functions as a central and recurring event that gives meaning to the author's pilgrimage through a world that is hostile to his religious convictions. One of the striking features of Shepard's self-writing is that it focuses less on the connection between the confessor's physical and spiritual states (for which Shepard reserved his *Journal*) than on the connection between illnesses of his family members and his own prospects for salvation. Early in the narrative, Shepard writes that, "I told the Lord his mercy should be the more woonderfull if in healing my child of his sicknes he would with all heale me of my sins" (Shepard 354).[4] Although many colonists believed that children were born sinful and continued to live in a state of utter depravity after birth, Shepard refuses to attribute his children's various sicknesses to original sin. Instead, he interprets them as punishments for his own iniquities. For instance, when one of his children suffers from a serious inflammation of the eyes, which Shepard describes in accordance with the medical parlance of his day, he concludes: "I must haue a blind child to be a constant sorrow to me till my death & was made to be contented to beare the indignation of the Lord because I had sinned resoluing now to feare nor care nor greeue no more, but to be thankfull nay to loue the Lords will" (356). Contrary to lay conversion narratives in which illness is most often configured as a point of entry for the confessor's initiation into knowledge, Shepard's text reveals that illness serves as a reminder of God's sovereignty, a renewal of the covenant, and as a blessing of the writer's ministerial endeavors.

Toward the end of his narrative these rather beneficial effects of illness are contrasted with a gloomy and truly morbid interpretation: when his wife dies in childbed, Shepard realizes that mounting afflictions lead to doubt and despair that require additional efforts to maintain faith in God. He therefore stresses the difficulty of seeing illness as a chance for personal improvement and as a source for consolation: "I saw that if I had profited by former afflictions of this nature I should not haue had this scourge; but I am the Lords, & he may doe with me what he will" (392). Shepard raises head-on a crucial point that most other personal narratives in colonial New England tend to avoid: if an

---

4   The notion that the illness of a family member functions as a punishment by proxy for the confessor's transgression is further detailed in the seventeenth-century conversion narratives of William Adams and Elizabeth Stacey (Strong 158, 163).

illness causes the seeker to enter into a covenant with God, then the next illness shows only the incompleteness and insincerity of the covenant and thus implicitly questions the providential purpose behind the previous affliction(s). For the Cambridge minister, this is not a case of theological inconsistency but rather a cause for propagating the imperfect nature of the human soul, its being constantly pulled away from the source of piety and morality toward the forces of darkness. Illness, as a cause for reform followed by doubt, despair, and backsliding is not depicted as a sign of God's indifference but rather as an intricate part of the Pilgrim's progress toward grace (cf. Colacurcio 105-147). What Shepard's autobiography and other similar Puritan texts necessarily have to omit—because they were written during adulthood, yet still well before death—is that a serious, perhaps final illness raises the problem of reform and backsliding to a much higher level of urgency. In other words, illness during adolescence or early adulthood is generally depicted as a stage prior to sanctification. The curious absence of sickness from later stages of life (and of the personal narrative), especially during old age, suggests that the integration of illness into a meaningful narrative of the self proved counter-productive to the pedagogical purpose of spiritual autobiographies.

III.

A third instructive example of the rhetoric of morbidity in Puritan personal narratives comes from the writings of Anne Bradstreet. For the Ipswich poet, a narrative account designed to instruct her children about life's difficult moments was of central importance. With "To My Dear Children," a letter written approximately three years prior to her death, Bradstreet composes a concise confessional narrative in which she aims to teach by example, showing how her assurance in religious and spiritual matters has been counter-balanced by phases of doubts about religion as such and her denomination in particular. The question of whether other denominations may store the true knowledge of, and path toward, salvation is answered by a return to the doctrines presented by Calvinist preachers in New England.

Among the lessons of life conveyed in her autobiographical letter, Bradstreet offers sound advice on how to deal with illness. In her early teens, she suffered under "a long fit of sickness which I had on my bed," and "often communed with my heart and made my supplication to the most High who set me free from that affliction" (Bradstreet 241). Illnesses continued to haunt the young English woman. After she recovered from smallpox at age sixteen, with a sense of having received a divine favor impossible to repay, her family emigrated to New England in 1630 on the *Arabella*, the flagship of the Winthrop fleet.

The representation of the migration to North America, a pivotal cultural and spiritual event in the lives of first-generation settlers, retains a tone of skepticism similar to that found in most lay conversion narratives. "I found a new world and new manners at which my heart rose," Bradstreet confesses her emotions upon arrival, but her misgivings and disgust about the "wilderness" soon give way to submitting to the Lord's will (241). Immediately following this famous passage, Bradstreet reflects on "a lingering sickness" that had been plaguing the soon-to-be mother since her arrival in the Bay Colony. For Bradstreet, writing in the privacy of her colonial home for almost four decades, it is less difficult to deal with personal illness than it is with the suffering of a child or grandchild. In all cases, however, the sufferer is to draw benefits from the illness. Because of the difficulties and insecurities they provide, illnesses constitute opportunities for spiritual growth: "sometimes he hath smote a child with a sickness, sometimes chastened by losses in estate, and these Times (through his great mercy) have been the times of my greatest getting and advantage" (242). The lesson of illness is announced in a fairly straightforward fashion: a sin committed or a duty neglected are the causes for affliction, which is a just act of punishment by God. Bradstreet's stance on illness, however, makes sense only when read in conjunction with her overall religious struggles, her rebellious thoughts and actions against God, and her consideration of atheism expressed in her autobiography (cf. Porterfield 11-113).

Aside from the letter to her children, Anne Bradstreet has left a number of other prose meditations on illness. The vignettes collected in the posthumously published "Andover Manuscript" also address posterity, presenting a speaker that teaches by example. Bradstreet repeatedly stresses her humble endurance when lying ill in bed. It is only in such a state of humility, she claims, that the examination of the self can usefully convene. Illness here illuminates the spiritual side of Bradstreet's being in ways that other similar revelatory moments (e.g., in prayer or during church service) lack. The function of illness is to survive it in order to be able to reflect on it in writing. The tool of language, the recovery not only of the body but also of the speaking/writing self, enables the final act of healing, a return to the world of language.

In her May 1657 entry after "a sore sickness," her reflection touches on practical and spiritual consequences of her illness-induced absence from the household of the family (255). Illness has rendered Bradstreet unable to perform the regular duties of a mother and housewife whose husband is frequently away on colonial business. It has made impossible the poet's calling in life and has, in doing so, denied her the main source of identity. Forcing the New England subject to radically examine itself in the sickroom, illness creates a state of exception from seventeenth-century gender and cultural norms. This state of exception ought to be reconfigured as a time of renewed self-fashioning, Bradstreet asserts. Precisely at the moment when human agency is threatened by a bodily distemper, the believer can turn to God and receive redemption and an opportunity to re-create her self in and through Christ. The key for Bradstreet is to accept that the decaying body actually signals its opposite: the flourishing of the soul. Punishment through illness is a desirable state of being and consciousness—"I can no more live without correction than without food"—essential as eating and breathing (257).

In another prose meditation, titled "May 11, 1661," after four years of relative health, Bradstreet once again meditates on a previous illness. This time her tone and mood are less optimistic than on previous occasions. Rather than integrating the illness into the evolving fabric of the Christian self, the poet now grapples with the insufficiency of (her) words. There is also a sense that the speaker finds her illness to be a cause for self-scrutiny but that the rules for behaving like a devout believer are increasingly difficult to live by. She hence asserts that if she were only able to use language properly, the praise for God would finally be "real." While being ill discontinues the existence of an economic agent producing material goods, it also enables the creation of a more spiritual self that produces mental and artistic values. These values are generated in the process of voicing human gratitude for regaining health in meaningful statements.

In this meditation on illness, Bradstreet not only reflects on bodily dysfunctions but also draws from them the rudiments of an aesthetic program. After recovery, she writes:

> I cannot render unto the Lord according to all His loving kindness, nor take the cup of salvation with thanksgiving as I ought to do. Lord, Thou that knowest all things know'st that I desire to testify my thankfulness not only in word, but in deed, that my conversation may speak that Thy vows are upon me. (259)

The speaker, in a self-reflexive instance, recognizes that words are not enough to express the full scope of gratitude for divine deliverance. The self-scrutiny during the preceding illness has granted insight into more proper and devotional behavior for the Christian pilgrim, and now the problem is how to represent this state of exception to God and the world. The final sentence outlines an aesthetic of gratitude based on the principle that writing constitutes a branch of human creativity spurred by the divine that can turn "word" into "deed." Bradstreet, in fact, considers a poem on the page as a "deed," a material offering and sacrifice written in gratitude and humility after recovery from illness.

By 1661, Bradstreet had developed a noticeable uneasiness with the fact that she was writing so frequently about illness, for each illness disproved or at least questioned the lessons learned by a previous affliction. Illness is morbidly threatening not only because it signals death, is accompanied by pain or marks a bodily dysfunction, but because it carries within it its inevitability and the promise of return. In short, there is no escape from illness. And this makes assigning meaning to illness all the more difficult for the New England colonist: once language seems to have "conquered" the body, illness reappears and confronts the self with a situation similar to the one it thought to have already successfully managed. Hence, similar to Shepard's autobiography, the believer needs to develop particular strategies for coping with the unpredictability, inevitability, and often fatality of sicknesses. For Bradstreet, one remedy lies in continually reflecting on illness and in producing poetry as testimonial offerings to God that look to the world as a theater of Providence that is designed to instruct believers by and during illness.

IV.

All of the autobiographical narratives studied here reflect the broad cultural dissemination of medical providentialism, the belief that God intervened in human affairs through matters of illness and healing, especially among his chosen few in New England. Medical providentialism shaped the course of colonial culture and society by instructing settlers how to deal conceptually with a variety of medical conditions. It inherently denied the efficacy of human intervention in disease affairs and stressed divine omnipotence as originator of all earthly afflictions. Seventeenth-century settlers placed a greater emphasis on attributing disease to God's immediate involvement than most of their European compatriots, for whom, in accordance with the Galenic tradition, the divine had encoded its medical power and wisdom in creation and thereafter had largely abstained from an intervention in human health affairs. This inscription of disease and medicine among early New Englanders is evident in many different colonial writings, among them travel and exploration narratives, letters, sermons, poems, and autobiographical texts. Among the most prominent self-narratives that illustrate the belief in medical providentialism is the short account by John Dane, a tailor from England who had come of age in Ipswich, New England.

In 1682, two years before his death, John Dane, a neighbor of the Bradstreets, recorded various interventions of divine providence and guidance in his life. His autobiography differs from the employment of soliloquy in most other New England spiritual narratives by adhering to the Augustinian model according to which the seeking subject engages in a dialogic relationship with God. In addition, Dane's use of vernacular phonetics creates a degree of improvisation and idiosyncrasy that is absent in most other contemporary personal writings. Unlike the autobiographies by members of the colonial elite (Winthrop, Shepard, Bradstreet, Mather), Dane's confession is a rare written self-narrative by a member of the laity. Perhaps owing to his social position, Dane emphasizes the struggle between a worldly self and a soul conditioned by New England orthodoxy in greater detail and with a more expressed talent for the literary than comparative Puritan authors (Neuman 252-254). Moreover, on the level of content, the individuality of experiencing divine guidance extends to the employment of illness that is linked more closely to behavioral transgression than in other New England spiritual autobiographies.

At one point in his self-narrative, Dane avoids church service and, instead, roams aimlessly through the countryside. Stung by an insect, his arm swells severely, leading Dane to interpret this as a sign of God's punishment for failing to attend the meeting. As the pain and swelling spread despite increased prayer, the narrator seeks the help of a surgeon who declines any medical advice and instead replies in the manner of an oracle: "I went to a surgin and askt him what it was. He said it was *the take*. I askt him what he meant. He said it was taken by the prouedens of god. This knoct home on my hart what my mother said, *god will find you out*. Now I made great promises that if god would here me this time I would Reforme" (Dane 151; emph. orig.). The metaphorical extension of the insect sting to a sting of remorse stresses a providential and spiritual reading of the physical condition. This motif is revisited at a later stage of the narrative when Dane reports of suffering from palsy, which once again raises his awareness of God's presence and guidance. A critical (and perhaps cynical) twenty-first-century observer trained in literary analysis can hardly overlook Dane's reference to how palsy affected his narrative abilities. The reader wonders whether Dane's palsy, "which did mutch weaking my brayne and spoyle my memory," has not turned him into an unreliable narrator who undermines the credibility of his redemptive spiritual relation as a whole (Dane 152). The assumption that the narrative becomes increasingly destabilized is further supported by Dane's presentation of an accumulation of events with providential resonances during his life journey rather than offering his reader substantial spiritual insights drawn from his experiences. Rather than an account of stereotypical introspection that one finds in other Puritan spiritual autobiographies, then, Dane merely claims that those who are tried and afflicted have a higher potential of receiving saving grace. In short, illness and other life calamities already signal salvation rather than triggering continual self-examination and reform.

V.

Boston minister and influential commentator on colonial life and theology, Increase Mather, was the busiest publicist among the autobiographers studied here. His many writings include a short narrative, which is similarly to other spiritual autobiographies designed to instruct the younger generation. Because of Mather's deep involvement in community affairs, it comes as no surprise that his text—part personal narrative, part political tract—unfolds the workings of God's intervention in his private life as well as in the larger course of New England. Mather's illness instructs the writing self and his audience not only about the meaning of distemper but also about means of recovery: as the author is inflicted with severe pain, fellow believers fast and pray, which restores his health. Omitting any reference to "secular" medical procedures, the Boston minister draws a causal relation between piety and healing, stressing that prayer constitutes the most efficacious and, in fact, the only remedy he needs to restore his health.

The adherence to prayer and fasting as a means of achieving and maintaining bodily and spiritual health, which is in keeping with larger cultural doctrines of healing in early New England, becomes more difficult to sustain when Mather describes his chronic case of hypochondria. Tormented by nightmares, then known as *epilates*, the author claims that the devil attempted to convince him that the nightly visitations were signs of madness, a diagnosis which causes Mather to fall into despair and melancholy (which presumably further fueled his being haunted by demons at night). To ease his increasingly morbid preoccupation with his physical and mental health, Mather undergoes an early form of hydrotherapy at the springs in Lynn, Massachusetts and finds solace and recovery in prayer and introspection. The perceived beginnings of madness are countered by a strikingly rationalized return to the healing guidelines embedded in Christianity: illness is the result of sin, Jesus died for human sin, and therefore recovery depends solely on repentance and full acceptance of Christ. Mather stresses that the restoration of his health will serve God, because only a healthy minister can spread the Word to others. Mather convinces his reader that, rather than having to submit to a long process of recovery, his soliloquy about Christian healing bears imminent fruits, ending this section with the words: "After prayer, I went away inwardly rejoicing, because *I have prevayled! I have prevayled! I have prevayled for mercy!*" (Mather 291). While the repetition of the words "I have prevayled" serves to claim the veracity of the patient's recovery, Mather actually attempts to finalize the healing process through speech acts. As the narrative continues Mather has to admit that recovery is slow and incomplete. During the following three months, he repeatedly concedes that the previous moments of remediation were delusional. Faced with the loss of faith, the minister can only admit his powerlessness and limitations *vis-à-vis* a sovereign God; however, rather than causing despair, this insight becomes the central pedagogical message for his reader:

> In the night I was vexed with troublesome dreames, and forced to rise before day. So that I now again was ready to conclude that my Ephialtes would issue in a Mania. But I went to God, and expressed my humble confidence before him that it should be otherwise, because hee heareth prayer, and because if this evil should come, those Truths of his which I have appeared for would suffer and because I desired to improve my understanding to his glory, therefore hee will contine it, though my sins deserve otherwise. (293)

Mather's continual suffering is not an indication that prayer has failed but rather a *cause* for humility and piety. The author constructs his literary persona as an ideal for other believers for whom a chronic illness might be an occasion to abide their faith. He hence elevates his personal experiences with disease into a model for his reader, showing, in hyperbolical terms, how a prominent minister is prone to doubt and despair, especially during occasions of sickness.

Mather's awareness of his personal and public selves, partly inherited, partly acquired during years of community service, permeates the fabric of the autobiographical or, rather, pathographical narrative. His spiritual relation includes illness not only as a state that draws the individual into a closer connection to God but also emphasizes that epidemics mark and shape the relations between the Puritan immigrant community and the divine. Commenting on the debate about the political motives and military strategies during King Philip's War (1675-1677), the Boston minister retrospectively informs his reader that,

> I was verily perswaded that God would punish that iniquity [i.e., public dissent over the war; M.P.] with some mortal disease, and accordingly I did in public 3 times declare as much, which some were troubled at me for but the Lord confirmed the work spoken, by sending mortal feavors which were epidemical, and the small pox also whereby many dyed. (302)

The smallpox epidemic during the war "preaches its own kind of sermon," with a clear religious and political message, Mather seems to be saying (Shea 162). Furthermore, he claims, the epidemic (as well as the initial Native American victories during the war) constitute providential signs of God's disappointment with the colonists' collective sins, especially backsliding and disrespect for the foundational covenant between the settlers and the divine. He then turns this religious reading into political demands, urging the Massachusetts General Court to punish and suppress sinful behavior. Smallpox, in other words, serves as an opportunity for Mather to claim his ministerial privilege of interpreting illness along theological trajectories. In doing so, disease becomes part and parcel of a political rhetoric that subsumes medical issues under the interpretive authority and remedial quality of religion.

Private self-scrutiny, made public, marked a central link in a broad array of personal narratives in seventeenth-century New England. In colonial American society, disease often sent the godly and the non-believers into the open, as it were, turning the individual over to the social. For most settlers, life in America, more so than in the mother country, demanded constant vigilance of the self, not only to gain assurance of individual salvation but also to erect and maintain a pious society that could serve as a (Winthropean) model for the rest of the world. In this introspective and intrusive culture, many colonists sought knowledge of their spiritual estates and of the condition of their bodies and endeavored to record their thoughts in writing. The inclusion of illness episodes in spiritual autobiographies—especially when steeped in morbidity—emphasized a recurrent theme in New England writings: the human helplessness *vis-à-vis* the natural world guided by the divine. Autobiographical writings functioned as literary extensions of the seminal and culture-shaping covenant which Puritans sought with God and with each other: they reflected on the manifestation of saving grace in the life of an individual and were energized by what many scholars have referred to as an "autobiographical pact," the agreement between author and reader about genuine truth claims presented by the author/narrator/character (Lejeune 119-137). Knowledge of the body was important because it entailed knowledge about the state of the soul and, therefore, the sustenance of the covenant. However, illness could only be rendered positively when bodily impairment was seen in correlation with spiritual advancement. Then, and only then, could the sinner hope to interpret the signs of illness as hints of imminent salvation.

Works Cited

Bradstreet, Anne. *The Works of Anne Bradstreet*. Ed. Jeannine Hensley. Cambridge: The Belknap Press of Harvard UP, 1967.

Cohen, I. Bernard. Ed. *Puritanism and the Rise of Modern Sciences: The Merton Thesis*. New Brunswick: Rutgers UP, 1990.

Colacurcio, Michael J. *Godly Letters: The Literature of the American Puritans*. Notre Dame: U of Notre Dame P, 2006.

Dane, John. "John Dane's Narrative, 1682." *New England Historical and Genealogical Register* 8 (1854): 147-156.

French, Roger and Andrew Wear. Ed. *The Medical Revolution of the Seventeenth Century*. New York: Cambridge UP, 1989.

Gonzalez-Crussi, Francisco. *A Short History of Medicine*. New York: Modern Library, 2008.

Grell, Ole Peter and Andrew Cunningham. Eds. *Medicine and Religion in Enlightenment Europe*. Burlington: Ashgate, 2007.

Magner, Lois N. *A History of Medicine*, 2nd ed. Boca Raton: Taylor & Francis, 2005.

Neuman, Meredith Marie. "Beyond Narrative: The Conversion Plot of John Dane's A Declaration of Remarkable Providences." *Early American Literature* 40.2 (2005): 251-277.

Lejeune, Phillipe. *On Autobiography*. Ed. Paul John Eakin. Minneapolis: U of Minnesota P, 1989.

Mather, Increase. "The Autobiography of Increase Mather." Ed. M. G. Hall. *Proceedings of the American Antiquarian Society* 71 (1962): 271-360.

Porterfield, Amanda. *Female Piety in Puritan New England*. New York: Oxford UP, 1992.

Shea, Daniel B., Jr. *Spiritual Autobiography in Early America*. Princeton: Princeton UP, 1968.

Shepard, Thomas. "The Autobiography of Thomas Shepard." Ed. Allyn Bailey Forbes. *Publications of the Colonial Society of Massachusetts* 27 (1932): 343-400.

Stoever, William K. B. "A faire and easie way to heaven:" *Covenant Theology and Antinomianism in Early Massachusetts*. Middletown: Wesleyan UP, 1978.

Strong, Robert, ed. "Two Seventeenth-Century Conversion Narratives from Ipswich, Massachusetts Bay Colony." *New England Quarterly* 82.1 (2009): 136-169.

Vickers, Brian. Ed. *Occult and Scientific Mentalities in the Renaissance*. Cambridge: Cambridge UP, 1984.

Webster, Charles. *From Paracelsus to Newton: Magic and the Making of Modern Science*. Cambridge: Cambridge UP, 1982.

Winship, Michael P. *The Times and Trials of Anne Hutchinson: Puritans Divided*. Lawrence: UP of Kansas, 2005.

Winthrop Papers. Vol. I. 1498-1628. Ed. Worthington C. Ford. Boston: Massachusetts Historical Society, 1929.

ARIANE SCHRÖDER

'Descent into Hell': The Cultural and Biomedical Signification of Depression in William Styron's *Darkness Visible*

> "The mind is its own place, and in itself can make a Heaven of Hell, a Hell of Heaven."
> John Milton, *Paradise Lost*

Lars von Trier's most recent movie *Melancholia* (2011) provides a very interesting cultural reading of clinical depression. Although a large part of the story depicts Trier's heroine Justine in a state of what would be typically understood as the symptoms of a severe depressive disorder (almost catatonic, she is unable to talk, eat or wash herself), when the film nears its inevitable catastrophic end (the earth will be extinguished by the meteorite *Melancholia*), the viewer witnesses a miraculous transformation. The closer the natural catastrophe, the calmer and more collected the depressive protagonist becomes. "Sick" Justine is suddenly the adept, whilst her "healthy" sister Claire is depicted as helpless. Von Trier does not present a stereotypical story of illness but rather develops through his reversal of agency a cultural reinterpretation of the biomedical disorder "depression."

This is one of many examples of how the biological fact of illness finds reverberation in our everyday life and culture. This paper will argue that the illness experience is always determined by its biological as well as its cultural "reality": while biological processes within the body are responsible for humans to fall ill, the individual's cultural environment is responsible for how he or she experiences that event. Illness thus can be interpreted as a dynamic and unstable process that is influenced by culture: shaped by time and space as well as by social and cultural markers such as race, class, gender, sexual orientation and religion. The binary structure of illness as culturally and biologically interdependent is mirrored in the illness autobiography that consists of both the master narrative on illness (its biomedical definition) and counter narratives (meanings generated by the ill subject and others). Exemplary for a multitude of illness narratives on depression, I will look at William Styron's autobiographical *Darkness Visible: A Memoir of Madness* (1990) and show how texts like his have the ability to represent the variety of meanings conveyed by this affliction as well as how illness autobiographies perpetually resist and reinforce common cultural and biomedical views on depression.

At the Crossroads of Biology and Culture

The experience of illness cannot be separated from the setting in which it takes place: its surrounding culture. In *Illness and Culture in the Postmodern Age* David B. Morris defines illness "as a mental, emotional, bodily event constructed at the crossroads of biology and culture" (19). A closer look at the etiology and meaning of clinical depression exemplarily reveals this form of biological and cultural interdependency. Kleinman and Good have pointed out that depression cannot be interpreted as an "universal disease" (2). The main reason for this is that "the study of depression continues to be plagued by unresolved conceptual problems" (ibid.). These problems manifest themselves at the root of culture: in terminology. The authors identify the term "depression" as simultaneously describing a "transitory mood or emotion," "a symptom associated with a variety of psychiatric disorders" and "a commonly diagnosed illness" (ibid.). Depression can thus be understood as an emotion or a disorder, it "simultaneously stands for two distinctive states of persons: one normal, the other pathological" (Kleinman and Good 8). If depression is perceived as "normal" or "pathological" varies greatly across cultures. Charles Keyes states that the mood is universal but not its manifestation or interpretation as illness (154). "Dysphoric" symptoms like sadness, hopelessness and lack of worldly pleasure are interpreted and expressed in strikingly different ways. For instance, the Western Judeo-Christian tradition emphasizes an overwhelming guilt and sinfulness that is associated with depression (as *acedia* or *melancholia* during the Middle Ages). Contrarily, Buddhist religion sees pleasure-seeking and happiness as the root of all suffering, thus depressive affect becomes "the first step on the road to salvation" (Kleinman and Good 3) and is highly appreciated. In Western societies, prolonged grief and dissociative behavior are often deemed pathological, other cultures, like the Kaluli of Papua New Guinea, "value full and dramatic expression of sadness and grieving" (ibid.) and interpret this as "normal" affect.

The matter becomes even more complex within the disorder "depression" itself. The disease can manifest itself in a large number of physical symptoms that could hardly be more unlike each other. While in the West typical symptoms include sleep, appetite and energy disturbances, in China many patients complain "of exhaustion of their nerves and of their hearts being squeezed and weighed down" (Kleinman and Good 4). Typical symptoms of depression in Nigeria include a sensation of "ants creeping in parts of the brain" (ibid.). With all these examples of cultural difference, how can the biomedical model convincingly claim that depression is merely a "neurotransmitter, neuroendocrine, and autonomic nervous system malfunction" (Kleinman and Good 9) treatable with a wide array of anti-depressives? The Western biomedical model is incapable of fully incorporating the complexity of depression: as emotion, symbol or disorder. Therefore a corrective—through individual perspectives or cultural analysis—is necessary.

Illness is a contested site at which the biomedical discourse tends to dominate all others. The advancement of modern medicine helped to extend human life and improve its general quality. Nevertheless its claim that medicine is the only answer to illness managed to virtually drown out all other voices on the subject, discrediting other perspectives as false or irrelevant. Arthur Frank has called this phenomenon "medicocentrism" (1997: 132): the marginalization of the patient's and other voices on illness in favor of the scientific biomedical discourse. The "power of the biomedical model" (Morris 5) can be exemplified by its use of language. Therefore, it is necessary to distinguish between "illness" and "disease" as socio-cultural categories. While disease is defined as "an objectively verified disorder of the bodily functions or systems, characterized by a recognizable cause and by an identifiable group of signs and symptoms," illness "is used inside medicine to indicate the patient's subjective experience, which may or may not indicate the presence of disease" (Morris 37). In this light "disease" appears to be a clean-cut objective category with a clear frame of reference, while "illness" refers to everything that is blurred by individual and subjective perception. This shows how already in language the voice of the patient is devalued, while the one of the medical professional is privileged.

Illness narratives attempt to break through this power hierarchy by voicing perspectives that the biomedical discourse discredits or silences. Corbin and Strauss have emphasized that our culture is in need of a "revision of the dominant medical imagery" (278) and Morris claims that the patient's perspective offers valuable insights that do not reject the biomedical model but complete it: "What biomedicine finds hard to recognize or to accept is that different observers—patient, spouse, doctor, [...] examining the same illness from their separate perspectives will observe different aspects of its truth" (5). Furthermore, Charles Keyes has argued that Cultural Studies and anthropology can provide a corrective or additional perspective to the biomedical model of "depression" because they understand it as "a cultural construct, one developed within but one particular cultural tradition—that of the West" (153).

Cultural Studies direct their attention to the intersection of the biological and cultural reality of illness. David Morris and Lennart Davis come to the conclusion that "[b]iology, as a science, cannot exist outside culture; culture, as a practice, cannot exist outside biology" (418). The analysis of illness' cultural implications is as vital to the subject as its biological or medical reality; therefore Cultural Studies have to have an interest in the study of illness. Kleinman and Good argue for "a dialectic approach that moves among and discloses the interactions between the concrete objective characteristics of human experience (both psychosocial and physiological) and their practical interpretation in a particular cultural tradition" (19).

Although one can understand illness as a cultural construction, the "reality" of illness and death is something we all need to face sooner or later. Therefore it is important to acknowledge that the cultural analysis of illness does not absolve us from the responsibility to honor and respect the reality of human suffering, as Stuart Hall has remarked (284-5). We can interpret illness as a cultural construction, claiming that its meaning is unpredictable and ever-changing and that the biomedical definition of illness is only one aspect of its truth but the reality of what it means to be living with depression cannot be left out of consideration. Paula Treichler argues that "[a]lthough meaning is indeed arbitrary and fluid, this does not mean that it is arbitrary and fluid within a given signifying system" because "[w]ithin the signifying system, that *is* the meaning" (173). After unmasking the medical reality of illness as constructed, cultural theory also has to tend to the "reality" of illness and the wide range of meanings it constantly creates.

Severe or life-threatening illness compels us to generate meaning. Why am I ill? What does it mean to be ill? Why me? Will I die? Am I responsible for my own illness? All those and many more questions arise in the event of illness and demand to be answered. The biomedical discourse is only partially able to provide answers. A patient with depression might ask himself whether his illness was brought on by a traumatic experience, whether he inherited the disposition from a depressive relative or if just some chemical imbalances in his brain are responsible for the onset of the disease. Nothing is more meaningless than illness and suffering, but we paradoxically still have to make sense of the event by assigning some form of meaning to it.

Of course, some illnesses are more prone to meaning-making processes than others. This phenomenon is directly linked to the biomedical reality of disease. As Susan Sontag points out, "[a]ny important disease whose causality is murky, and for which treatment is ineffectual, tends to be awash in significance" (58). Since there is no definite cure for depression in sight, and biomedicine and psychology cannot agree on a definite cause for the disease, it remains threatening and able to create new patterns of meaning. The analytical work for Cultural Studies of illness is not to judge credibility but to look at the intersection of biology and culture in order to collect all those meanings and ask why certain metaphors become attached to an illness in favor of others.

Culture influences how illness is experienced, but illness also leaves imprints on culture. David Morris has tried to show how different diseases have vitally influenced societies throughout history. For example, the Renaissance is in his view marked by the rise of an obscure illness that caused severe lethargy and suicidal madness that became known as "melancholia" at the time. Although this condition was already known to Hippocrates and later explained by Galen's Four-Humor-Theory as an excess of black bile in the organic system, it was only during the Renaissance that melancholia turned into a dangerous public threat that could virtually affect anyone (54).

It would be convincing to declare depression to be the defining illness of Western civilization at end of the 20th and beginning of the 21st century. Statistics show a steady increase in depression cases and depression-related syndromes like neurasthenia or the infamous "burn out." But the same is also true for a number of other diseases such as cancer, HIV/AIDS or coronary heart disease. All of them seem to have a hold upon society but none of them could be singled out as the most influential. What all of them have in common though, and what Morris understands as the defining feature of our age is that they all are chronic and gradually debilitating conditions. Due to the advances of modern medicine, in this part of the world infectious diseases that kill quickly appear to belong to the past. Illness has become an isolated event in an individual's life that needs to be integrated and lived with. Many patients are part of what Arthur Frank has called the "remission society" (1995: 8): even when they recover from their bouts with these diseases they have to live in permanent fear of the return of their affliction. This causes a permanent shift from short-termed pain towards long-lasting suffering. Illness autobiographies can provide a creative outlet to alleviate such individual suffering inflicted by the traumatic experience of chronic disease.

Illness Autobiographies: Disruption, Reconstruction and Continuity

Ida Cermak has described the experience of severe illness as a "three-front-war": it compels one to cope with illness-related pain and other debilitating symptoms, to deal with the repercussions it inflicts on relationships to others and to come to terms with the recognition of one's own mortality and eventual death (100). But not only has the patient to be present at these three fronts at the same time, he or she also has to face the new and disturbing self-image which illness projects: it "threatens to undo our sense of who we are" and "constitutes an immersion in an alien reality where almost everything changes" (Morris 22). Severe and especially permanent chronic illness can be interpreted as a traumatic event that invariably changes the patient's life, relationships, priorities and outlook on life itself. It has often been compared to the effect of a natural catastrophe; it certainly shares with it the notion of complete helplessness, shock and desperation.

Michael Bury argues that "the development of a chronic illness [...] is most usefully regarded as a 'critical situation,' a form of biographical disruption" (169). But the illness experience does not only influence and (maybe permanently) change our lifestyle, it affects our idea of self, the root of the identity we have built for ourselves.[1] "Selfhood is the product of an internal

---

1   I am aware that many cultural theorists, especially postcolonial theorists, would argue that there exists no such thing as one "identity." Here, I work with the sociological idea of "identity of sameness," which implies that intact health constitutes a stable identity that is fragmented through the traumatic experience of severe illness.

autobiography; identity hangs by a narrative thread" (Couser 17), thus illness disrupts our self-narrative, posing the threat of "identity spread" (Conrad 11). When identity "spreads" our self becomes fragmented: the "who-I-was" is not the "who-I-am" and what could possibly become of "who-I-will-be"? The question that arises is which methods do patients employ in order to reassemble their shattered or fragmented understanding of self after the impact of chronic illness like depression? Arthur Frank believes that the key to the reestablishment of an integrated whole is narrating one's own illness experience (1995: 53).

Gareth Williams, building on Bury's work, has called the process of self-repair through storytelling "narrative reconstruction" (177). He claims that it "is an attempt to reconstitute and repair ruptures between body, self, and world by linking-up and interpreting different aspects of biography in order to realign present and past and self with society" (197). Narrative reconstruction primarily takes place through conversations with doctors, family members and friends or during moments of self-reflection. Since these musings are in themselves fractured because they are permanently interrupted through health regimens and other daily activities the patient has to follow, one could speak of many short stories; this also explains the text's often fragmentary and ambiguous character.

In order to reestablish a form of temporality in a disrupted life narrative, illness autobiographies can provide "narrative continuity" (Rimmon-Kenan 2002), because they manage to realign the patient's past, present and possible future by means of a coherent and complete story. Rimmon-Kenan notes that written illness narratives "restructure past memories and future expectations in a way that would cohere with the present, bridging the gap by creating a new kind of continuity" (2002: 13). The self-image of the patient is thus gradually reshaped by highlighting different life aspects of the past and new plans for the future with the present reality of being chronically ill. The fractured narrative identity is repaired by placing it within a new context: traumas and crises experienced and lived through in the past are connected with the present occurrence of chronic illness, thus turning the latter into "one more episode in a recurrent structure, with the additional value of hope" (Rimmon-Kenan 2002: 16). Through the narrative illness can be integrated into life as only one event within a succession of hardships that have been overcome.

But not only does the illness narrative provide "narrative continuity" within the self-story it also constitutes "something new—it does not merely reflect a self-perpetuating pathological process. What is new is that "suffering is given a form" (Hydén 56). But writing about a disaster such as severe illness does not only help us to overcome fragmentation and shifts the focus towards individual suffering, it also "gives shape to who we are. It does not destroy us, but it inscribes us. [...] Out of the struggle with the disaster and the attempt to give it a voice, we, in the process shape our own voice" (Awalt 17). Hence, stories about illness invite us to consider that the illness experience could indeed be interpreted as a natural part of life and not as a scandal or catastrophe that isolates one from the "healthy" others.[2]

Illness constantly generates meaning making processes. Illness autobiographies provide a super-structure that places the diverse array of meanings within the context of a story. Ilka Kangas claims that illness narratives can be understood as "both a tool and a result in the process of making sense of illness where the meaning of illness is contextualized" (76). The narrative provides the structural pattern for illness meanings and the complete text itself can be seen as a commentary, the product of a self-reflection on the subject. After being confronted with the multitude of meanings, illness autobiographies offer the chance to select meanings that seem most appropriate to the "wounded story-teller." This selection process can be understood as a form of empowerment since "this is an act of creative choice in an area of life where choice and creativity are almost wholly denied" (Hawkins 90).

But how do writers choose those meanings? At this point it is useful to employ the concept of the "master narrative" in this selection process. John Stephens defines it as "a global or totalizing cultural narrative schema, which orders and explains knowledge and experience" (7). In *The Postmodern Condition: A Report on Knowledge* (1979) Jean-François Lyotard criticizes the idea of "grand" or "master narratives" such as Christianity and argues that they have instead been replaced by smaller "local" narratives, "petits récits" (11-13). If we understand the biomedical definition of a disease as a master narrative, all its cultural meanings represent local or counter narratives. While the biomedical discourse is still valid and present (like all other "grand narratives"), Lyotard is correct in assuming that they have lost their persuasive strength. Yet their influence has only been diminished, not completely extinguished and new and challenging counter narratives of illness are created.

Nevertheless, counter narratives cannot operate completely outside of the realm of the master narrative. Thus, illness autobiographies always remain at least partially faithful to the meaning of the master narrative because it provides guidance. One can compare this relativity to a patient's medical compliance: one individual might strictly obey every rule the doctor imposes, while another only follows prescriptions that appear sensible to him or her. Michael Bamberg concludes that narrators "never totally step outside the dominating framework of the master narrative, but always remain complicit and work with components and parts of the existent frame 'from within'" (363). However, the authors of those texts are also capable of creating counter narratives that intentionally challenge certain aspects of the master narrative. What Jonathan

---

2 Since the beginnings of life-writing, with the works of St. Augustine, the main focus of these texts was a turning point, a moment of conversion that divides narrative time into a "before" and "after." For illness autobiographies this turning point is marked by the onset of a chronic affliction.

Raskin claims for autobiographies in general is also true for stories of illness. He argues that people who are aware of "cultural constructions" can also actively resist and manipulate those forms of meaning through combination and alteration (320). Illness autobiographies perpetually reinforce and challenge the hegemonic master narrative of illness.

The way an illness autobiography is situated between master and counter narratives mirrors the illness experience itself, which takes also place within a dichotomy, namely between the realms of biology and culture. Since illness is never purely cultural or biological, the story about illness is never fully dominated by the master or the counter narrative. All elements merge in a synthesis that, taken as a whole, makes up the written illness experience: "The detailed empirical and symbolic particularities of this life trajectories, like those of every other, create a unique texture of meaning—external layers written over internal ones to form a palimpsest—for each person's experience of chronic illness" (Kleinman 32). Within this palimpsest the boundaries between distinct entities blur, but fractures and contradictions remain clearly visible. The often conflicting character of these texts responds to the fragmentation of the self that illness inflicts on the chronically ill: "In ill subjects (and perhaps not only in them), this process [of narrative structuring] contains phases of disintegration and fragmentation as well as moments pulling toward continuity and coherence, and these may even be simultaneous" (Rimmon-Kenan 2002: 22).

Rimmon-Kenan also claims that there is a felt tension between the topic and the form of an illness autobiography. While on the one hand the story concerns itself with describing how illness causes the disintegration of the self, a falling apart of one's inner and outer world, the text provides the narrative stability and control that the story-teller craves. Hence, the illness autobiography as a whole oscillates between acknowledging fragmentation (through the contents of the story) and trying to overcome it (by writing the story) (2006: 244). This fluctuation between the governing principles of the text, fragmentation and order, is what causes the often contradictory nature of illness autobiographies. Additionally, the perpetual reinforcement of and resistance against the master narrative on illness also leads to conflicting perspectives within the text.

Another aspect that differentiates stories of illness from autobiography in general is that they are "narratives forever in search of meaning," as Lars-Christer Hydén has pointed out. He considers illness narratives as a "continual negotiation" in which meaning is "constantly changing and being renegotiated, depending on changing perspectives and other changes in the illness process" (61). Although every text is formally bound to terminate at some point, illness autobiographies are stories with an open end. A closure to the story often does not lie within the realm of the text but is only found outside of it. William Styron's text cannot convey that he would have recurring depressive episodes after the publication of *Darkness Visible*. However, illness narratives are not about closure but about opening up. They offer storytellers the opportunity to find continuity by integrating illness into their life and although they might not be in control of the ending of their story they receive the chance to acknowledge and accept their fate.

Darkness Visible

William Styron was already an acclaimed writer of several novels such as *The Confessions of Nat Turner* (1967) and *Sophie's Choice* (1979) when he published *Darkness Visible – A Memoir of Madness* (1990), an autobiographical text about his struggle with severe depression. It chronicles a depressive episode that eventually led to the author's admittance to a closed psychiatric ward because he was at the risk of suicide. His illness narrative is a "recovery story" —he writes from the supposedly secure vantage point of the ex-patient, as a member of the "remission society." The memoir consists of ten chapters that roughly describe the chronology of events from the onset of the illness until his recovery nine months later. Already the first sentence sets the tone for the whole narrative: "In Paris on a chilly evening late in October of 1985 I first became fully aware that the struggle with the disorder in my mind—a struggle which had engaged me for several months—might have a fatal outcome" (3). Styron establishes his text at once as an illness autobiography. Although he does not use the words "depression," "death" or "suicide," the reader immediately understands that the I-narrator suffers from an illness that is severe and might be life-threatening.[3]

The author's illness autobiography touches upon a variety of issues and problems relating to depression, but he also tries to find expressions for an illness that manifests itself mainly in the sufferer's head. In my analysis I will focus on the way the author generates meaning from depression: the losses it entails, how the Christian imagery of hell can be employed to describe it, how mental suffering can be reconfigured as physical pain, how biomedicine writes itself back into his text and finally, how William Styron finds a way to repair his shattered identity.

The feeling of loss is immanent in almost every illness narrative, *Darkness Visible* provides a vivid example: "Loss in all of its manifestations is the touchstone of depression—in the progress of the disease and, most likely, in its origin" (Styron 56). Throughout Styron's text the concept of loss manifests itself in various parts of his disintegrating identity, he feels deprived of his artistic ability, of his self-confidence and hope, and finally, of his will to live. The author notes the lack of certain mental and physical abilities already at an early stage of the illness; it represents a shift that marks the onset of his depression.

---

3 It is important to note that Styron's depressive episode took place at a time when medical knowledge on the disease was still very vague. Prozac, the most successful anti-depressant so far, was only released in 1987, two years after his first encounter with the illness.

He claims that his "surroundings took on a different tone at certain times" and often experiences "a kind of panic and anxiety" as well as "a visceral queasiness" (42). As the illness progresses, the I-narrator experiences more and more difficulty in simply enjoying his life. But depression does not only affect his mood but also his physical state: "I felt a kind of numbness, an enervation, but more particularly an odd fragility—as if my body had actually become frail, hypersensitive and somehow disjointed and clumsy, lacking normal coordination" (43).

With his mood and physical state deteriorating Styron is incapable of maintaining a normal life but his identity is further threatened: "[...] the act of writing itself, becoming more and more difficult and exhausting, stalled, then finally ceased" (46). An author who cannot write is not an author anymore: his profession defines his identity and his illness leaves him unable to "perform" this idea of identity. The loss of ability becomes especially painful because one does not lose the memory of what one was once capable of. Styron's achievements as a writer were a constant reminder of his changed state that left him without the possibility to express his frustration or anguish. His incapacity furthermore led to a lack of confidence; since he could not live up to his own expectations as a writer, friend, father or husband, he considered himself worthless (5). This feeling increases because the I-narrator becomes more and more incapable of socially interacting with others. The loss of identity that is initiated through the loss of ability and confidence leads to the loss of the author's humanity. He feels alienated, "like an automaton" (59) and when confronted by others he says that "[...] I would respond like the zombie I had become" (19).

Susan Sontag states that "[t]he most terrifying illnesses are those perceived not just as lethal but as dehumanizing, literally so" (126). In this sense, for Styron, depression is such a terrifying illness because his condition forces him to behave in ways that are contradictory towards his own understanding of himself and his humanity. This loss is further exemplified by Styron's use of war metaphors. Interestingly, he does not use them to describe his fight against his illness (he is in no condition to do so) but he sees himself as a "walking wounded" soldier who cannot cope with his situation: "The sufferer [...] finds himself, like a walking casualty of war, thrust into the most intolerable social and family situations. There he must, despite the anguish devouring his brain, present a face approximating the one that is associated with ordinary events and companionship" (62-3). Styron does not see himself as a warrior, who fights his illness, but rather as a victim of war—he is not active but passive—depression is dominating all aspects of his life.

The dehumanizing aspects of his illness lead the author to also lose all sense of hope for recovery:

> In depression this faith in deliverance, in ultimate restoration, is absent. The pain is unrelenting, and what makes the condition intolerable is the foreknowledge that no

remedy will […]. If there is mild relief, one knows that it is only temporary; more pain will follow. It is hopelessness even more than pain that crushes the soul. (62)

While being stupefied by his illness, Styron's mind still senses that his life is passing him by. This is what makes depression so dreadful: the fact that one is still aware of the loss one is experiencing through the illness. The author feels the inappropriateness of his mood and behavioral patterns but cannot do anything to change them. He comes to the conclusion that "if depression had no termination, then suicide would, indeed, be the only remedy" (84). Styron believes that his identity has been destroyed by the illness and he has no hope that this situation will change. His decision to end his life is not only based on the fact that he cannot stand the pain any longer but also in the belief that he is just "finishing" depression's destructive work: his body is useless, his mind cannot focus on his tasks, he is incapable of social interaction with others, so what else is there to destroy, if he is already almost dead? His attempt at self-destruction is materialized through his notebook. It contains his most intimate thoughts that he shares with no one else. Styron comes to the following conclusion: "So as my illness worsened I rather queasily realized that if I once decided to get rid of the notebook that moment would necessarily coincide with my decision to put an end to myself" (59). The notebook becomes his self—if he destroys it, it is the first step in the direction of complete self-annihilation.

The notebook also represents the linearity of his life story; a form of order amidst the chaos the depression has thrown him into. If he eradicates the notebook he also lets the chaos of depression take full command over his being. During one evening in December he finally decides to get rid off it and his *modus operandi* underlines his self-deprecation: he puts it into an empty cereal box and throws it away like garbage. "Fire would have destroyed it faster, but in garbage there was an annihilation of self appropriate, as always, to melancholia's fecund self-humiliation" (64). Although he has thrown away his innermost thoughts he cannot bring himself to finally take his life—after all, the notebook is just a notebook—shortly after this incident he commits himself to a psychiatric ward in order to hold on to the only thing he still has left: life.

But *Darkness Visible* focuses not only on the mental and physical damages that depression can inflict but the author consciously contextualizes the illness within a Western cultural paradigm. For instance, his memoir refers to John Milton's description of hell in *Paradise Lost:*

> No light, but rather darkness visible / Served only to discover sights of woe, / Regions of sorrow, doleful shades, where peace / And rest can never dwell, hope never comes / That comes to all, but torture without end / Still urges, and a fiery deluge, fed / With ever-burning sulphur unconsumed. (Book I: 63-69)

Milton depicts hell as a place of utter hopelessness and anguish; it evokes a feeling of desperation and anxiety, which is reverberated in Styron's own words when he describes his suffering:

> [D]espair, owing to some evil trick played upon the sick brain by the inhabiting psyche, comes to resemble the diabolical discomfort of being imprisoned in a fiercely overheated room. And because no breeze stirs this cauldron, because there is no escape from this smothering confinement, it is entirely natural that the victim begins to think ceaselessly of oblivion. (50)

He uses Christian imagery of hell: unbearable heat, the devil stirring his cauldron. The place of banishment for the lost souls is typically characterized as tormenting its inhabitants with excruciating pain and at the same time withdrawing from them all sense of hope. Being in hell means suffering for eternity —suffering from depression equals that state because the I-narrator has also lost all hope of recovery: "I had now reached that phase of the disorder where all sense of hope had vanished [...]" (58). But the equation of hell and depression has a severe flaw: in the Christian belief system, only sinners are condemned to the torment of eternal hell—this would involuntarily put blame on the sufferer.

Styron evades this pitfall by also referring to Dante Alighieri's *Divine Comedy* (1308-1321). He directly quotes from the first canto of "The Inferno" in which the hero, accompanied by the ancient poet Virgil, descends into hell: "In the middle of the journey of our life / I found myself in a dark wood, / For I had lost the right path" (82). And he concludes his narrative by Dante's last canto from "The Inferno" in which the young explorer ascends from the hell fires again into the light: "And so we came forth, and once again beheld the stars." (84) It is essential to note that Dante is only a visitor to "the Inferno"— he descends into the darkest depths of hell but he does not have to stay. He only observes and describes the sinners' suffering. Styron creates an equation between his own struggle with depression and Dante's journey into the darkness. Both are poets who descended into hell and managed to come back and share their tale: "For those who have dwelt in depression's dark wood, and known its inexplicable agony, their return from the abyss is not unlike the ascent of the poet, trudging upward and upward out of hell's black depths and at last emerging into what he saw as 'the shining world'" (84).

By using both Milton and Dante in creating his representation of depression as hell, Styron manages to produce an image of suffering without putting blame on the sufferer. He combines the agony of Milton's hell with Dante's position of the visiting observer. Thus, the hell of depression remains a place of torment but one that also offers the hope of return to "the shining world" (Styron 84). This understanding of hell corresponds to Susan Sontag's concept of health and illness as "dual citizenship": "Although we all prefer to use only the good passport, sooner or later each of us is obliged, at least for a spell, to identify ourselves as citizens of that other place" (3). For Styron "that other place," Sontag's "kingdom of the sick," is represented by "hell." But the references to Dante's *Divine Comedy* are not only linked to "The Inferno" but also to the two other places the poet visits during his journey: purgatory and heaven. William Styron again finds comparable structures in his own narrative. After he has acknowledged that he needs medical help in order to overcome his illness he says: "The hospital was a way station, a purgatory" (69). And during his recovery period in the hospital when he finally begins to feel better, he describes this improvement as an ascent into heaven: "[…] although I was still shaky I knew I had emerged into light. I felt myself no longer a husk but a body with some of the body's sweet juices stirring again. I had my first dream in many months, […]" (75). If for the author hell resembles illness, then heaven is equated with his restored health. The imagery of "the Inferno" as metaphor for Styron's condition is important because there are two aspects that give the concept of hell its torturous character: the unrelenting agony and the complete absence of hope for improvement. The author claims that this is exactly what makes depression so terrible: the unrelenting psychological and physical pain and the belief that one will never recover. Nevertheless, like Dante's hero in *The Divine Comedy*, he manages to convalesce and "emerge into the light" (75) again.

When trying to verbally express what pain means and feels like one reaches the limits of representability. Often the sufferer has to resort to preverbal utterances like moans, screams and crying. Elaine Scarry explains this phenomenon: "Physical pain does not simply resist language but actively destroys it, bringing about an immediate reversion to a state anterior to language, to the sounds and cries a human being makes before language is learned" (4). In its immediate presence pain is barely communicable—but what about memories of pain, accounts of pain experienced in the past? One of the most pressing matters for William Styron in writing down his "memoir of madness" is to illuminate the fact that the pain inflicted by depression is not only psychological but physical as well. He argues that pain is one of the major reasons why people with depression eventually commit suicide in order to terminate their agony. He tries to find words for the indescribable: the pain he endured while suffering from a severe episode of depression. He laments the "basic inability of healthy people to imagine a form of torment so alien to everyday experience" and describes the pain as "most closely connected to drowning or suffocation—but even these images are off the mark" (17). Styron believes that others could better acknowledge the illness' physical torment if one could find the appropriate words for it. As an author he is aware of the difficulty to manifest pain in language but the images he evokes resemble what is generally considered a "hard death" and make the depressive's suicidal thoughts more comprehensible for the observer.

The problem of pain as a symptom of clinical depression is imminent in the whole discussion of the illness in Styron's narrative for two reasons: he wants to establish the illness as a physical as well as a mental disease in order to free depressive patients from the stigma that surrounds their death. Styron tries to show that suicide is the common progression of the illness if a patient does not receive appropriate help[4] because suicide remains one of the most severely stigmatized forms of death. The author hopes that if people learn to see that the pain of the depressed patient is so severe that life becomes hell, they would understand that for some, suicide is the only way out of their agony: "the pain of severe depression is quite unimaginable to those who have not suffered it, and it kills in many instances because its anguish can no longer be borne" (33).

At the beginning of his narrative the author states that he is "a kind of autodidact in medicine" (9), he has always been interested in medicine in general and read several medical textbooks. Therefore it is not surprising that throughout his narrative Styron employs biomedical discourse rhetoric to represent his illness: "depression in its major stages possesses no quickly available remedy: failure of alleviation is one of the most distressing factors of the disorder as it reveals itself to the victim, and one that helps situate it squarely in the category of grave diseases" (10). He often uses medical terminology to describe his condition but acknowledges at the same time that modern medicine still has insufficient knowledge of the causes and treatments for clinical depression.

Styron's opinion on medicine is profoundly ambiguous. On the one hand he is deeply entangled in the medical discourse, especially when he speaks about pharmaceuticals (71). On the other hand he remains always critical, especially towards his psychiatrist. He describes the relationship to his doctor as highly problematic: "I felt a bit like Emma Bovary in my relationship with the psychiatrist I shall call Dr. Gold, whom I began to visit immediately after my return from Paris, when the despair had commenced its merciless daily drumming" (51). Styron compares Emma Bovary's relationship to the local priest with his relationship to Dr. Gold: both he and Flaubert's heroine seek help in their mental distress, both receive no consolation. The priest has only "Christian platitudes" (ibid.) to offer to Emma and the doctor can only provide Styron with medical commonplaces. The author sees the comparison of her fate with his own as appropriate because Emma kills herself at the end and he is on the verge of committing suicide. In Styron's opinion, Dr. Gold has failed him and he holds him partly responsible for the dwindling of his health. The author's ambiguousness towards biomedicine and health care makes him an ideal example of the interdependency of biology and culture and show in how far the master narrative of biomedicine overlaps with his own counter narrative on the illness experience.

---

4 According to the American Foundation for Suicide Prevention (AFSP), 36.000 U.S. Americans die from suicide every year. Almost 90 % of them "have a diagnosable and treatable psychiatric illnesses—such as major depression, bipolar depression, or some other depressive illness."

Styron's outlook on hospitalization differs from most illness narratives. While many patients cannot wait to leave the supposedly sickening atmosphere of the hospital ward, Styron embraces it. For him it is a place of healing, a safe haven that prevents him from taking his life. He interprets the hospital as his "salvation" because he "found the repose, the assuagement of the tempest in my brain, that [he] was unable to find in [his] quiet farmhouse" (69). The hospital provides him with order and the "gratifying trauma of sudden stabilization" (ibid.)—the common saying that "it is hospitals that make you sick" is contrasted by Styron's narration. This is especially unusual under the circumstance that the author does not experience his healing process in an "ordinary" hospital but in a closed psychiatric ward, one of the most abject places within Western culture. Interestingly, Styron does not bolster the popular stereotypical view of the "mental asylum" as for instance depicted in Ken Kesey's *One Flew over the Cuckoo's Nest* (1962). He explicitly admits himself to a psychiatric institution against Dr. Gold's advice who had told him that "I should try to avoid the hospital at all costs, owing to the stigma I might suffer" (67-8). The doctor's advice is seen as counterproductive to the patient's wellbeing; Styron feels that his physician focuses on such a minor problem as social stigma in the face of an acute life-threatening illness. This example underlines how the biocultural entanglement also can affect health care professionals: here, Dr. Gold bases his advice not on biomedical fact but cultural stereotype. The question of social stigma is most immanent when trying to cope with depression. Whether it is suicide as an option to end the agony, or admitting that one has serious mental health problems, the general public's reaction towards the mentally ill is often predetermined and biased. Styron acts against his doctor's opinion and is open about his condition because he feels that absolute honesty is a precondition in the process of coping and healing.

Reestablishing Identity

Darkness Visible is for a large part concerned with the difficult fates of many famous artists. In several chapters Styron speculates on the mental state of such figures as Albert Camus, Randall Jarrell, Abbie Hoffman or Italo Calvino. He argues that all of them have suffered from a similar condition: clinical depression. He identifies a connection between artistic talent and the occurrence of depression, similar to Kay Redfield Jamison's arguments in *Touched with Fire: Manic-Depressive Illness and the Artistic Temperament* (1993). He claims that "artistic types are particularly vulnerable to the disorder—which, in its graver, clinical manifestation takes upward of twenty percent of its victims by way of suicide" (35). William Styron not only finds consolation in comparing his fate with literary figures such as Madame Bovary or Dante's alter ego but also by drawing connections between himself and historical or contemporary artists who were supposedly suffering from depression. He takes comfort in the fact that there is a link between great artistic talent—in his repetitive lists of artists one can find such renowned names as Virginia Woolf, Vincent van Gogh, Ernest Hemingway, Sylvia Plath, Paul Celan and others—because it reassures him as an artist whose creativity has been impaired and his identity has been severely threatened by this illness. While Styron suffered from depression he could not write, the loss of his creative ability had a huge impact on the author's confidence and his understanding of himself as a writer. By comparing his condition to that of other artists he is able to reconstruct his seemingly lost identity. The illness that had suddenly destroyed his personality becomes incorporated into his life story. Thus, Styron's personal bout with depression turns into a feature in his vita that he shares with other artists: creativity and depression seem to be interrelated and his illness finally makes sense, at least in the way that it makes him who he is. He manages to rebuilt his lost identity and strengthen his self-confidence through this connection.

An illness narrative does not only chronicle the catastrophic event of a severe illness but gives the author the chance to reinterpret his life under the changed circumstances. In William Styron's case, he not only reconsiders his identity as an artist but also reflects upon his literary work in the light of depression, realizing that suicide had been a constant motif in his novels and that the illness "had clung close to the outer edges of my life for many years" (78). For Styron, incorporating the illness into his life means to reflect upon the changes it imprints on the present and the future as well as on the past. Although depression had only recently afflicted him, he believes that it had been always present, enabling him to create convincing character studies of people suffering from that affliction. Again, Styron uses his illness to win something back that depression had taken from him. Although he was unable to write while suffering from depression, he believes that the illness' permanent presence in the background made his most successful literary work possible. He incorporates the disease into his identity by assigning it partial responsibility for his artistic talent.

While William Styron tries to grasp the meaning of depression in his life he gives an accurate depiction of the common contemporary assumptions on depression. But he also provides his audience with a sufferer's perspective on the affliction. The author attempts to defeat certain stereotypes that surround the illness while reinforcing others. He struggles to find appropriate words for his suffering but he does not lose hope that at some point the cultural, together with the biomedical discourse, will be able to fully grasp the meaning of this mysterious condition.

Von Trier's *Melancholia* or Styron's *Darkness Visible* remind us that it is necessary to challenge the hierarchical structures within the discourse on illness, so as to show that health care professionals do not have more authority on the issue of depression than patients or family members. In order to attend to the suffering of someone afflicted with depression, there has to be awareness not only of the dangers of "medicocentrism" but also of the "free-floating" cultural stereotypes that surround the illness experience. Here, Cultural Studies can provide an analytical link that collects and interprets the elements of a "culture of illness" to establish a model that puts the ill individual and his or her suffering at the center of attention.

Works Cited

Awalt, H. Mike. "Writing the Disaster: Inscriptions of the Self." *Suffering, Death and Identity*. Eds. Robert N. Fisher, Daniel T. Primozic et al. Amsterdam, New York: Rodopi, 2002. 5-18.

Bamberg, Michael. "Considering counter narratives." *Considering Counter-Narratives. Narrating, resisting, making sense*. Eds. Michael Bamberg, and Molly Andrews. Amsterdam and Philadelphia: John Benjamins Publishing Company, 2004. 351-371.

Bury, Michael. "Chronic Illness as Biographical Disruption." *Sociology of Health and Illness*, 4.2 (1982): 167-182.

Cermak, Ida. *Ich klage nicht. Begegnungen mit der Krankheit in Selbstzeugnissen schöpferischer Menschen*. Wien: Amalthea, 1972.

Conrad, Peter. "The Experience of Illness: Recent and New Directions." *Research in the Sociology of Healthcare: The Experience and Management of Chronic Illness*. Eds. Julius A. Roth and Peter Conrad. Greenwich (Conn.) and London: Jai Press, 1987. 1-32.

Corbin, Juliet and Anselm L. Strauss. "Accompaniments of Chronic Illness: Changes in Body, Self, Biography, and Biographical Time." *Research in the Sociology of Healthcare: The Experience and Management of Chronic Illness*. Eds. Julius A. Roth, and Peter Conrad. Greenwich (Conn.) and London: Jai Press, 1987. 249-282.

Couser, G. Thomas. *Altered Egos. Authority in American Autobiography*. New York and Oxford: Oxford UP, 1989.

Davis, Lennart J. and David B. Morris. "Biocultures Manifesto." *New Literary History*, 38 (2007): 411-418.

Frank, Arthur W. *The Wounded Storyteller: Body, Illness and Ethics*. Chicago: CUP, 1995.

---. "Illness as moral occasion: restoring agency to ill people." *Health*, 1.2 (1997): 131-148.

Hall, Stuart. "Cultural Studies and Its Theoretical Legacies." *Cultural Studies*. Eds. Lawrence Grossberg, Cary Nelson, and Paula Treichler. New York and London: Routledge, 1992. 277-285.

Hawkins, Anne Hunsaker. *Reconstructing Illness: Studies in Pathographies.* West Lafayette: Purdue UP, 1993.

Hydén, Lars-Christer. "Illness and Narrative." *Sociology of Health and Illness.* Vol.19, No.1 (1997): 48-69.

Jamison, Kay Redfield. *Touched with Fire. Manic-Depressive Illness and the Artistic Temperament.* New York: Free Press, 1993.

Kangas, Ilka. "Making Sense of Depression: Perceptions of Melancholia in Lay Narratives." *Health* 5.1 (2001): 76-92.

Keyes, Charles S. "The Interpretive Basis of Depression." *Culture and Depression. Studies in the Anthropology and Cross-Cultural Psychiatry of Affect and Disorder.* Eds. Arthur Kleinman, and Byron Good. Berkeley and Los Angeles: University of California Press, 1984. 153-174.

Kesey, Ken. *One Flew Over The Cuckoos Nest.* 17th repr. New York: Viking Press, 1962.

Kleinman, Arthur and Byron Good. "Culture and Depression." *Culture and Depression. Studies in the Anthropology and Cross-Cultural Psychiatry of Affect and Disorder.* Eds. Arthur Kleinman, and Byron Good. Berkeley and Los Angeles: University of California Press, 1984. 1-33.

Kleinman, Arthur: *The Illness Narratives. Suffering, Healing and the Human Condition.* New York: Basic Books, 1988.

Lyotard, Jean-François. *The Postmodern Condition: A Report on Knowledge.* Trans. Geoffrey Bennington, and Brian Massumi. Minneapolis: University of Minnesota Press, 1984.

Milton, John. *Paradise Lost.* Philadelphia: Hayes & Zell, 1854.

Morris, David B. *Illness and Culture in the Postmodern Age.* Berkeley, Los Angeles: University of California Press, 1998.

Raskin, Jonathan D. "Constructing the narrative unconscious." *Considering Counter-Narratives. Narrating, resisting, making sense.* Eds. Michael Bamberg and Molly Andrews. Amsterdam and Philadelphia: John Benjamins Publishing Company, 2004. 317-323.

Rimmon-Kenan, Shlomith. "The Story of 'I': Illness and Narrative Identity," *Narrative,* 10.1 (2002): 9-27.

---. "What Can Narrative Theory Learn From Illness Narratives?" *Literature and Medicine,* 25.2 (2006): 241-254.

Scarry, Elaine. *The Body in Pain. The Making and Unmaking of the World.* New York: Oxford UP, 1985.

Sontag, Susan. *Illness as Metaphor and AIDS and Its Metaphors.* New York: Picador, 1990.

Stephens, John. *Retelling Stories, Framing Culture : Traditional Story and Metanarratives in Children's Literature.* New York: Garland, 1998.

Styron, William. *Darkness Visible. A Memoir of Madness.* New York: Random House, 1990.

Treichler, Paula. *How to Have Theory in an Epidemic. Cultural Chronicles of AIDS*. Durham: Duke UP, 2006.
Williams, Gareth. "The Genesis of Chronic Illness: Narrative Reconstruction." *Sociology of Health and Illness*, 6.2 (1984): 175-200.

AESTHETICS OF DEATH

SANDRA POPPE

The Aesthetics of Death and Mourning in American Literature and Film

Introduction

What would it be like to leave behind one's own life and never come back? How can the passage between life and death even be imagined and what does the finiteness of life imply? Since the beginning of time, this have been questions pondered by mankind, but until now they have found no concrete answer. Though death can be experienced, this experience excludes its communication. No one can tell what happens in the moment of death and after. This ignorance causes fear and insecurity regarding the imagination of one's own death. According to several leading academics, such as the French historian Philippe Ariès, thoughts of death are consequently excluded from everyday life, particularly since the beginning of the twentieth century:

> In our day, in approximately a third of a century, we have witnessed a brutal revolution in traditional ideas and feelings, a revolution so brutal that social observers have not failed to be struck by it. It is really an absolutely unheard-of phenomenon. Death, so omnipresent in the past that it was familiar, would be effaced, would disappear. It would become shameful and forbidden. (85)

Ariès attributes this development mainly to the influence of the United States throughout the Western World:

> It seems that the modern attitude toward death, that is to say the interdiction of death in order to preserve happiness, was born in the United States around the beginning of the twentieth century. (94)

For this radical and partly simplified position Ariès has quite often been the subject of criticism. Whether one follows his argumentation or not it seems in either case obvious that such a supposed taboo of death does not apply to literature, the arts and media—especially the uncertainty of death and the anxiety involved constitute a specific challenge to artists and filmmakers.

Whereas one's own death cannot be anticipated, experienced or conveyed, the loss of another person can be communicated. Among the effort to imagine the perspective of a dying person, there are plenty of artistic works depicting the perspective of the bereaved. The topic of death and in particular of mourning is the main subject of this paper. With the description of mourning and grief we are entering a special field of artistic preoccupation: the depiction of emotions. Grief is an emotional reaction belonging to the primary emotions of mankind (Strasser 39). As existential emotions are a common subject of art works the description and presentation of grief as a liminal experience often occurs in literary texts as well as in other art forms.

The aim of artistic preoccupation with such existential feelings is to depict the inconceivability of the definite loss. This depiction can fulfill several functions concerning the recipient: The identification and empathy with a fictional character involved in an existential situation can lead to an emotional comprehension of this situation. This emotional experience does not take place in the unprotected space of real life but at a secure distance to the fictional world described. Thomas Anz points out the pedagogical effect of such a reception. From the safe distance of reception the reader or film viewer tentatively feels what it is like to go through emotions such as loss, grief and pain. In contrast to 'real feelings' these feelings provoked by the reception of fiction remain without consequences requiring action. The qualities Thomas Anz finds in literary texts and their reception can also be consigned to other media such as film, painting and music (Suckfüll 234-235; Wulff 31). In a similar way this possibility is also given to the artist in the very moment he creates his work: Within the safety of aesthetic distance the artist also has the opportunity to deal with existential subjects and to 'test' several emotions connected with these subjects. This possibility to tentatively approach feelings that are avoided in everyday life provides an answer to the question why the preoccupation with death and grief persists into the presence.

The cultural scientist Thomas Macho points out a new visibility of death (Macho 26) in the arts and media. Considering the great success of the HBO-series *Six feet under* in the United States, one is tempted to agree with Macho. The same can be said about the autobiographical text *The Year of Magical Thinking* (2005) by Joan Didion in which she writes about the sudden death of her husband. Both producers and recipients seem to have a serious interest in dealing with this subject, which has been treated as taboo for a long time.

Based on selected examples from American literature, film and TV-production, I would like to show the types of artistic and aesthetic dealings with death and mourning found in recent literary and cinematic productions. I will examine different possibilities to depict death and grief in the media and various options of interpretation available to us to analyse these artefacts. Therefore, several current examples have been chosen in order to illustrate different aspects of the subject: Joan Didion's autobiographical text mentioned above, Don DeLillo's short novel *The Body Artist* (2001), the HBO-series *Six feet under* by Alan Ball and the film *The Fountain* (2006) by Darren Aronofsky.

Joan Didion's *The Year of Magical Thinking*

In *The Year of Magical Thinking* Joan Didion describes her own reaction to and the dealing with the death of her husband John Gregory Dunne as well as the serious illness of her daughter Quintana Roo, who died after the publication of the text. The title of the text is an allusion to the year following the death of Didion's husband. This year is determined by different phases of grief Didion is undergoing. She describes these phases in a partly emotional, but mostly rational and self-reflective mode. A dominant assertion in her account is the following: "Life changes fast. Life changes in the instant. You sit down to dinner and life as you know it ends" (Didion 3). These are the opening sentences of the book and the first Didion writes after the death of her husband. At the same time they function as a kind of leitmotif-assertion, which recurs throughout the whole text. They point out the unexpected intrusion of death in everyday life. Didion is unprepared for her husband's death; she feels helpless and unable to face the situation.

Her first reaction is to recapitulate the incident in order to categorize it as a fact of reality. At the same time she is trying to delay this coming to reality by not informing friends and family immediately; only a day after his death does Didion find the strength to communicate her husband's death to others: "[…] but I needed that first night to be alone. I needed to be alone so that he could come back. This was the beginning of my year of magical thinking" (Didion 33). This assertion shows an irrationality of thinking and feeling connected with the wish that the incident of John's death might be temporary and not conclusive. The hope that John would come back is stronger than a rational comprehension of the incident. Although Didion is acting and reflecting as a reasonable adult, she is not able to completely realize her loss: "[…] I was incapable of thinking rationally. I was thinking as small children think, as if my thoughts or wishes had the power to reverse the narrative, change the outcome" (Didion 35). This way of 'magical thinking' goes so far that it begins to influence Didion's behaviour: "I could not give away the rest of his shoes. I stood there for a moment, then realized why: he would need shoes if he was to return. The recognition of this thought by no means eradicated the thought" (Didion 37). This passage clearly shows that emotion or irrationality and cognition or rationality do not exclude each other but are closely linked in the case of Didion's depiction. This connection of emotion, with its cognitive reflection, is an important characteristic of the text considering that emotion and cognition have been regarded as opposites for a long time in the philosophical and theoretical preoccupation with feelings (Winko 333-335.).

Another example that shows how feeling and the reflection of emotions are connected is the naming and analyzing of bodily sensations and reactions:

> Tightness in the throat.
>
> Choking, need for sighing.
>
> Such waves [waves of grief; S.P.] began for me on the morning of December 31, 2003, seven or eight hours after the fact, when I woke alone in the apartment. I do not remember crying the night before; I had entered at the moment it happened a kind of shock in which the only thought I allowed myself was that there must be certain things I needed to do. (Didion 28)

The emotional and irrational state of mind is described as 'grief' while Didion calls the wilful and rational consideration of her loss 'mourning'. During this consciously practiced mourning Didion is reflecting upon the transience and limitation of human life.

> We are imperfect human beings, aware of that mortality even if we push it away, failed by our very complication, so wired that when we mourn our losses we also mourn, for better or worse, ourselves. As we were. As we are no longer. As we will one day not be at all. (Didion 198)

With this discussion of mortality she points to the central aspect of time and its perception which are closely linked to the topics of death and loss. The passing of time which brings us closer to the end of life, is always connected with transience. But in the process of mourning the passing of time can equally have a positive, healing effect: pain caused by loss is fading and the development from emotional grief to conscious mourning can take place. Time and the passing of time are central in Didion's text, which brings us back to the title of the book: *The Year of Magical Thinking*. For one year Didion holds on to the irrational hope that her husband might eventually come back to her. This year is determined by her memories of John, but this phase is ended abruptly by the first anniversary of his death.

> I realize as I write this that I do not want to finish this account. Nor did I want to finish the year. [...] I realized today for the first time that my memory of this day a year ago is a memory that does not involve John. This day a year ago was December 31, 2003. John did not see this day a year ago. John was dead. (Didion 225)

Once more this passage shows the cardinal function of this so-called "magical thinking" which suppresses the pain of loss that is at the moment too great to be endured—the irrationality of magical thinking functions therefore as a kind of protective mechanism. With the end of this illusion a new stadium of mourning begins: acceptance. According to Elisabeth Kübler-Ross, who worked on the subject of death and grief, every confrontation with death and loss has to end with acceptance. Kübler-Ross differentiates five phases of emotional occupation with one's own death: denial and isolation, anger, bargaining, depression, acceptance (cf. Kübler-Ross 51-146). Even if Kübler-Ross develops her phases in consideration of people who are concerned with their own death, her differentiation is transferable to the situation of people dealing with the loss of close relatives (cf. also Strasser 40-41). Each phase can be found in Didion's account. The phases sometimes overlap, sometimes alternate in her description. This variation is mainly a result of the constant connection of emotion and cognition that characterizes Didion's account. With this combination of reflection and description of emotion she gives the reader the opportunity to identify with the described feelings of being overpowered and helpless in the confrontation with an outrageous situation. At the same time she manages to distance the reader from this experience by the reflective explanation of these feelings. Thomas Anz's argumentation that the possibility of participation and distance simultaneously pushes the reader to face existential feelings in the arts is confirmed by Didion's text and its popularity.

Don DeLillo's *The Body Artist*

Don DeLillo's short novel *The Body Artist* delineates a similar situation: a woman loses her husband. The 36-year-old performance artist Lauren Hartke is shocked by the suicide of her husband, the 64-year-old and formerly celebrated filmmaker Rey Robles. Deeply traumatized, Lauren Hartke searches for ways to handle her loss. The described attitude and conduct of Lauren completely differs from the one described by Joan Didion. Comparing the texts, one has to take into consideration that DeLillo's text is purely fictional, whereas Didion's account is autobiographical. As the title *The Body Artist* already announces, DeLillo describes mainly a physical acting out of grief and emotion. However, like in the case of Didion, the topics of suppression and acceptance of death in relation to the passing of time are central within this depiction.

Lauren's first reaction after the death of her husband is isolation. She retreats into a secluded house located at the sea which she and her husband had rented for some months; she does not answer the telephone; she communicates with no one, not even with herself. That means she ignores the emotional reactions regarding the death of her husband. She distracts herself with housekeeping instead. But Lauren soon discovers a strange cohabitant on the third floor of the building, a male being that she can neither classify in age nor in provenance or character.

> He was smallish and fine-bodied and at first she thought he was a kid, sandy-haired and roused from deep sleep, or medicated maybe. [...] He looked at her and seemed older now, the scant act of head-raising, a simple tilt of chin and eyes that was minutely crucial to his transformation – older and faintly moist, a sheen across his forehead and cheeks. (DeLillo 43, 45)

Mr. Tuttle—as the visitor is called by Lauren—communicates exclusively through the reproduction of snippets of communication and gestures, interchanged by Lauren and Rey before his death.

Many critics have been puzzled by the character of this figure, which was interpreted partly as a real person inside the fiction, partly as a product of

Lauren's imagination. The most conclusive interpretation is given by Laura di Pretes who suggests that Mr. Tuttle can be understood as an embodiment of trauma and with it as a fantasy figure of Lauren's subconscious. At the same time Di Pretes interprets Mr. Tuttle as "embodied voice" and "speaking body" through which Lauren's suppressed grief is articulated (501). 'Embodied voice' denotes the vocal imitation given by Mr. Tuttle. 'Speaking body' refers to Mr. Tuttle's physical expression that can also be understood as an allusion to Lauren's condition. After the loss she feels alienated from her own body: "Her body felt different to her in ways she did not understand. Tight, framed, she didn't know exactly. Slightly foreign and unfamiliar. Different, thinner, didn't matter" (DeLillo 35). It is precisely this foreignness as an expression of deep shock which is embodied by Mr. Tuttle and his appearance. DeLillo points out the central function of the body in a situation of shock: The body acts out the loss even before it can be mentally and emotionally comprehended.

In the following Lauren begins to adapt her own body to the one of Mr. Tuttle; and by doing this she is achieving a bodily and artistic (in the sense of performance art) processing of her loss and grief. This metamorphosis appears as a radical and painful process.

> She wax-stripped hair from her armpits and legs. It came ripping off in cold sizzles. She had an acid exfoliating cream, hard-core, prescribed, and after she stripped the hair she rubbed in the cream to remove wastepapery skin in flakes and scales and little rolling boluses that she liked to hold between her fingers and imagine, unmorbidly, as the cell death of something inside her. (DeLillo 85f.)

Lauren is performing changes of her body that can be understood as a reduction or even a negation of her corporal individuality.

> This was her work, to disappear from all her former venues of aspect and bearing and to become a blankness, a body slate erased of every past resemblance. [...]. In the mirror she wanted to see someone who is classically unseen, the person you are trained to look through, bled of familiar effect, a spook in the night static of every public toilet. (DeLillo 86)

Two needs are expressed by this corporal metamorphosis: on the one hand to make clear the irrevocable fact of the loss that cuts Lauren from all that has been before; on the other hand it shows the desire to vanish, to exist no more: "She wanted to disappear in Rey's smoke, be dead, be him" (DeLillo 36). However, this metamorphosis turns out to be productive, because the artist Lauren is going to act it out as a stage performance in front of her audience. This acting out gives her the chance to realize something in public that she could not handle in private. In her performance Lauren embodies different figures; one of these figures is unmistakably Mr. Tuttle whom she imitates vocally. That seems to be a paradox because Mr. Tuttle imitated her and Rey in voice and gesture at first. But then it becomes coherent: By embodying Mr.

Tuttle, who himself is an embodiment of her own trauma, she at last accepts this trauma and thereby also her grief.

The way to this acceptance is again deeply connected with time and the passing of time. The title of the performance Lauren is enacting, points exactly to the connection of physicality and temporality: *Bodytime*. Both Mr. Tuttle and Lauren seem to be unrelated and unfixed concerning time. This absence of temporal orientation can be understood as a reaction to the traumatic loss and a suppression of the connected emotions. Presence is omitted whenever it is possible, because a deliberate experience of presence would require an acceptance of the loss. In turn, without the acceptance of these negative feelings there is no way to get over them.

> Time is the only narrative that matters. It stretches events and makes it possible for us to suffer and come out of it and see death happen and come out of it. But not for him [Mr. Tuttle]. He is in another structure, another culture, where time is something like itself, sheer and bare, empty of shelter. (DeLillo 94)

By enacting her performance Lauren executes this condition of temporal disorientation on stage. She cannot return to herself and her loss until this point of corporal and mental zero-point is accomplished. Similar to the phases described by Didion, Lauren also undergoes several stages of trauma and grief that finally lead to acceptance.

> Why not sink into it? Let death bring you down. Give death its way. Why shouldn't the death of a person you love bring you into lurid ruin? […] Why shouldn't his death bring you into some total scandal of garment-rending grief? Why should you accommodate his death? Or surrender to it in thin-lipped tasteful bereavement? Why give him up if you can walk along the hall and find a way to place him within reach? Sink lower, she thought. Let it bring you down. Go where it takes you. (DeLillo 118)

Only this final acceptance of pain and grief that can even mean loss of control is able to bring Lauren back to herself. However, it was this eventuality of loss of control that led to a suppression of pain and grief before. Now that she has faced pain and loss, Lauren can remember her dead husband without the need of Mr. Tuttle as a medium. With this her perception of time and time flowing returns: "She threw the window open. She didn't know why she did this. Then she knew. She wanted to feel the sea tang on her face and the flow of time in her body, to tell her who she was" (DeLillo 126). This last sentence of the novel brings together the perception of time with the sensation of the body and in so doing leads to an arrival in the presence.

Whereas Didion points out the connection and sometimes also confrontation of emotion and cognition/reflection, DeLillo describes the enactment of a traumatic experience through the body. The ways of dealing with loss and grief proposed by Didion and DeLillo are totally different, although there are several similar aspects in both texts such as the importance of time and the passing of time or the attempt to isolate oneself and to suppress the events:

Didion focuses on her ability to reflect and express her thoughts, feelings and perceptions through the medium of language. DeLillo depicts a character that acts much more intuitionally on a corporal level, which mistrusts verbal language and makes it dispensable at the same time. Thereby DeLillo shows that loss can be beyond comprehension to an extent that the rational medium of verbal language fails to capture the emotion. The body artist Lauren seems to show that the bodily expression can be a more natural, more intuitional possibility of expression in an extensional situation such as loss and grief.

Both examples show that there are different options of treating the subject of death and mourning in literature: Through direct and rational reflection as well as through metamorphosis and personification of an imagined character. At this point of the argumentation one might ask about possibilities open to the cinematic medium to express emotions that sometimes are beyond rational treatment. This question is going to be answered with the help of two completely different examples: the HBO-series *Six feet under* and the film *The fountain* by Darren Aronofsky.

Alan Ball's *Six feet under*

The TV-series *Six feet under* focuses on the Fisher family living in California and running a funeral home. Throughout the serial several members of the family are going to die. Furthermore, every episode narrates the death of a person who is going to be embalmed and entombed in the funeral home. In contrast to the literary examples the depiction of death in this filmic example is characterized by concrete visibility. Each episode starts by showing the death of a person followed by the reconstruction of his body for a viewing with an open casket in the funeral home. Especially the non-American viewer learns much about the practices of burial in the United States, where it is common to honour the deceased at his or her open casket. For this special moment the deceased is embalmed and made up, giving the impression that he is sleeping rather than dead. This practice is criticized several times throughout the series. It is alluded to that such practice may suppress the reality of death and transience.

In the following, some sections of the first and the last episode will be examined more closely in order to compare them to aspects and motives already analyzed within the literary examples. Especially the first episode treats a central subject already found in the literary texts: the brutal and unexpected impact of death on everyday life. The head of the Fisher family dies in a car accident on Christmas Day. His death hits the family unprepared despite their everyday confrontation with the shocks and losses of other bereaved. This first episode shows each family member at the moment of hearing the news of the father's death; each of these situations changes radically with the intrusion of the news: The daughter, Claire, is taking drugs with other high school kids and all of a sudden becomes aware of her narcotized and drugged condition (S 1, E

1 00:09:23-00:11:41); the son, Nate, has just had sexual intercourse with a stranger in the lumber-room at an airport as he receives the news (S1, E1 00:08:01-00:09:22). The emotional reaction of the mother and wife, Ruth Fisher, is depicted most intensively: described as a 'control freak' by her son Nate she sustains a nervous breakdown at hearing the news of her husband's death. Crying and screaming, she hurls her Christmas roast across the kitchen and, for a moment, loses control and is overwhelmed with emotions (S. 1, E 1, 00:07:00-00:08:00). This scene already shows the directness with which emotions can be depicted in the filmic media by the acting, mimic and gestures of the actors. The approach to the emotions depicted seems to be more direct for the viewer, rather than emotions described through literary language.

The characters of Ruth Fisher as well as her son Nate depict the fluctuation between a dutiful conduct in daily routine, a mourning appropriate to the conventions and a breaking free from these conventions. Only this breaking free of conventions allows a direct acting out of emotions such as pain and grief. The most concrete sequence in the first season is the funeral, which takes place at a cemetery and is moderated by a priest who prays and drops some earth on the casket with the aid of a little castor. At first, Nate is refusing to follow this habit, commenting how silly the whole ceremony appears to him: "It is like he's salting popcorn" (S. 1, E. 1, 00:48:13-00:50:03). Affected by his reactions, Ruth is breaking out in cries and sobs and at the same time grabs the earth of the tomb and throws it on the casket (S. 1, E. 1, 00:50:09-00:51:20). The filmic representation of death is marked by a concrete visualization as well as a direct enacting of emotions connected to loss. The more concrete modes of representing the thematic aspects linked to the subjects of loss and grief, for example the oscillation between conventional conduct and outbreak, is also mentioned in the texts of Didion and DeLillo.

Didion's text is characterized by a strong connection between emotion and reflection; in DeLillo's novel this connection is replaced by an enacting of emotion through the body or bodily expression. It then seems interesting to know, if these aspects are also relevant in the filmic depiction as well. Especially the corporal aspect of death, but also of grief, is present in the serial. The already mentioned reconstruction and embalming of corpses often shown in the serial is one aspect of this. The bodily enactment of grief is primarily depicted by the interpretation of the actors: for example in the emotional breakdown of the mother, Ruth Fisher. These are pictures that convey the emotional condition of a character without requiring any further comment. But what about the possibility of reflecting emotions in the filmic medium?

Critics have often denied the possibility of reflection and even commentary in film. For example the film critic George Bluestone postulates:

> The film, by arranging external signs for our visual perception, or by presenting us with dialogue, can lead us to infer thought. But it cannot show us thought directly. It can show us characters thinking, feeling, and speaking, but it cannot show us their thoughts and feelings. A film is not thought; it is perceived. (48)

This denial ignores the variety of stylistic means of expression the film possesses to reflect and comment. Especially in *Six feet under* the depiction of emotions and the reflection of them is closely linked. In situations of high emotional intensity or in situations of delicate emotions the serial operates with a special technique to depict the inner dialogue of the character acting: The deceased appear to the characters and are speaking their thoughts out loud. An example can be found in the first episode when Nate has to identify his dead father who is lying on a stretcher before him (S. 1, E. 1, 00:18:04-00:18:48). Nate hesitates and all of a sudden the father stands in front of him and explains to him his fear as a result of being faced with death and his attempts to suppress something that has to be accepted because it is part of everyday life. In this manner emotion and reflection are connected by the appearance of the deceased and their speaking out loud the emotions and thoughts of the living. This is an appropriate method, because it is clear to the viewer that the apparition of the deceased can only be understood as a visualization of the acting character's thoughts.

With this technique of visualizing the emotions and thoughts through the apparition of the deceased, Alan Ball creates a convincing technique which allows him to integrate the depiction and reflection on the level of action. The subject of fear regarding one's own mortality, provoked by the confrontation with the death of a family member or friend, is described by Didion in detail. It is also taken up by the film sequence mentioned above. Exactly this aspect of one's own mortality and the momentariness of life is taken up centrally in the last episode of the serial. The youngest protagonist, Claire Fisher, sees her own future path of life as well as that of her loved ones just until their death as well as her own death in a kind of time-lapse flash-forward. These flash-forward scenes are cleverly cut in the present scene, where one sees Claire in a kind of fast motion driving out of town into the open land (S. 5, E. 12, 01:00:05-01:06:02). Both the depiction of passing time and human mortality is conveyed by this last sequence of the serial. At the same time, Ball succeeds in handling these delicate subjects in a conciliatory way. Here, as well as in the texts of DeLillo and Didion, the end of the story is marked by the acceptance of one's own possibility of death.

Darren Aronofsky's *The Fountain*

The last example of this analysis, Darren Aronofsky's film *The Fountain*, completely differs from the direct and realistic depiction of death and grief in the serial *Six feet under*. Though the visibility and visuality of death and grief is also central in *The Fountain*, it is staged on a metaphorical, symbolical, metaphysical and even fantastical level. Moreover, Aronofsky treats further subjects connected with the own death as well as the death of others, such as the perception of death as a healable disease. The hubris of the human being who tends to control life and death is thus one of the aspects taken up by Aronofsky. He confronts this position with the belief in rebirth, connected with the presumption that new life can only arise from past life. He thereby creates two completely contrary positions which he confronts on several time and plot levels. In each case the two contrary positions are embodied by a female (Rachel Weisz) and a male (Hugh Jackman) character—a couple that struggles with love, death and caducity on each level. Once more, time plays an important role in this construction.

The first plot line is situated in Spain at the beginning of the 16th century: Queen Isabel sends out her conquistador Tomas to Guatemala with the mission to secure for her an elixir of the tree of life that shall give her eternal life. This deed seems to her the only opportunity to stop the upcoming inquisition. She gives a ring to Tomas and promises to be his wife upon his successful return. Tomas reaches the tree of life after a dangerous fight with its keepers and first drinks from the elixir himself. Confident of victory he tries to put on the ring Isabel gave him, but at the same moment he is transformed by an abrupt metamorphosis into a meadow of flowers (01:23:14-01:23:44). His resurrection is accomplished, because he will live on—but at the same time he ceases to exist as a human being. Thus the idea of immortality is confirmed, but on the other hand the condition of this resurrection is revealed: Immortality can only be reached through the vanishing of the momentary appearance—no resurrection can take place without this 'death'. This idea is variegated on the two other time levels.

On the second time level—Canada in the year 2000—the medic Tommy fights feverishly for the life of his incurably ill wife Izzy. She has resigned to her own death by studying the Mayan myth of creation which is based on the belief that a new life is born only by the death of another creature. The star Shibalba that creates thousands of new stars by his explosion is a symbol for this. Izzy is not able to convince Tommy of her belief: Instead of spending time with her and listening to her, he is working in his laboratory without a break. His aim is to create an elixir for Izzy that he tests endlessly on an ape. Only after her death he is able to engage in the idea of caducity and eternity, which he learns of in a book Izzy had written before her death. This book is also the link to the first time level, because it is Izzy who writes the story of Queen Isabel and the conquistador Tomas. As a symbol of his understanding Tommy plants a tree on Izzy's grave (01:25:35-01:2625).

This tree not only serves as a link to the first but also to the third time level. It is situated in the year 2500 in a free-floating bubble that can be understood as a depiction of the star Shibalba. The inner space of the bubble is dominated by a dying tree and an ascetic who is trying to save the tree. This salvation of the tree does not succeed until the ascetic understands that he has to sacrifice himself and the tree in order to gain eternal life. This sequence is the most fantastical and the most visual of the film. As suggested by Izzy regarding the star Shibalba, the bubble with the tree and the ascetic in it explodes into a thousand golden pieces in order to merge with eternity (01:24:35-01:25:10).

In this last sequence the ring, as a symbol of the union of the lovers, reappears: The ring, which Tomas did not manage to put on before his metamorphosis (01:22:56-01:23:07), the ring that Tommy lost in his laboratory (00:18:21-00:18:42), the ring that the ascetic finally puts on his finger before merging with the cosmic Nirvana (01:23:55-01:24:29). The way to eternity is hereby completed and the lovers are reunited—even if they no longer exist in their former appearance. The different time levels, which are not narrated chronologically throughout the film, are also connected in this last image of the film. All three episodes retell the same love story in different variations and all of them develop towards an acceptance of mortality and caducity as well as an acceptance of the faith in resurrection. Traditional symbols, such as the fountain of youth already mentioned in the film title, the tree of life, the metaphor of travel or the symbol of the ring are hereby used as leitmotifs. The topic of medical treatment and the involved attempt to combat death like an illness that can be healed instead of accepting it as a natural end of life is still prevailing. In Aronofsky's film this topic is connected with the ancient aspiration for immortality, which is in turn confronted with the paradox that immortality can only be reached by accepting one's own caducity and resurrection in death—this being the only way to contemplate the life cycle. In the film the story of eternal love narrated throughout the centuries is constructed as a kind of alternative idea to the one of corporal immortality deemed to be impossible.

Some aspects already mentioned in the analysis of the other examples also manifest in Aronofsky's film such as temporality, visuality, emotion. However, *The Fountain* is special in the outline of these aspects: Aronofsky depicts a temporality that confronts caducity with eternity, a visuality that does not aim for a concrete presentation of death and the deceased but for a visualisation of a mystical conception of non-volatility. The depiction of emotions is mainly connected to the love and grief of the male figure for the female figure. The connection between emotion and reflection found in the other examples is not relevant in *The Fountain*. The emotion of grief is confronted with another entity: faith—a faith in caducity as part of the life circle described in the old Mayan myths. Again, similar to the other examples *The Fountain* displays the need to accept one's own mortality, being faced with the death of the other.

Conclusion

A main criterion besides the relative actuality of the examples analysed was their variety concerning the depiction of death and grief. However, what seems to be a common characteristic is revealed by the denouement of the examples. Each work ends with the acceptance of death and grief and a kind of conciliation with the fact of caducity. This appears to be relevant especially against the background of the often-cited assumption that modernity in the Western world is marked by a suppression of death. In spite of its popularity, this statement has often been criticized. It becomes evident that, even if one wants to follow the argumentation of Ariès, it is not accurate for the artistic preoccupation with the topic of death. On the contrary: literature and film seem to offer an opportunity to deal with the topics of grief and death which are suppressed in everyday life.

Agreeing with Thomas Macho one is tempted not only to proclaim a new visibility of death, but also a new conciliation with death and grief—at least in literature and film. This aesthetic activity offers the chance to deal with the subjects of death and grief through the safe environment of fiction. The occupation with literature and film depicting death and grief not only offers the possibility to live through existential feelings in the safe setting of fiction, it also allows the adoption of a certain acceptance of death and caducity—eventually also with regard to one's own life and death.

Works Cited

Anz, Thomas. "Freuden aus Leiden. Aspekte der Lust an literarischer Trauer." *Freiburger literaturpsychologische Gespräche. Jahrbuch für Literatur und Psychoanalyse* 22 (2003): 71-82.

Ariès, Philippe. *Western attitudes toward Death from the middle ages to the present.* Trans. Patricia M. Ranum. Baltimore/London: The Johns Hopkins University Press, 1975.

Bluestone, George. *Novels into Film.* Baltimore: The Johns Hopkins Univ. Press, 1957.

DeLillo, Don. *The Body Artist.* New York/London et.al.: Scribner Paperback Fiction 2002.

di Prete, Laura. "Don DeLillo's The Body Artist: Performing the Body, Narrating Trauma." *Contemporary Literature* 46/3 (2005). 483-510.

Didion, Joan. *The Year of Magical Thinking.* London: Harper Perennial, 2006.

Kübler-Ross, Elisabeth. *On Death and Dying.* New York: Simon & Schuster, 1997.

Macho, Thomas. "Die Wiederkehr der Toten nach der Moderne." *Six feet under. Ausstellungskatalog.* Ed. Kunstmuseum Bern. Leipzig: Kerber, 2006. 15-27.

Six Feet Under. Dir. Alan Ball. Perf. Peter Krause, Michael C. Hall, Frances Conroy and Lauren Ambrose. Home Box Office. 2001-2005.

Strasser, Petra. "Trauer versus Melancholie aus psychoanalytischer Sicht." *Freiburger literaturpsychologische Gespräche. Jahrbuch für Literatur und Psychoanalyse* 22 (2003): 35-52.

Suckfüll, Monika. "Emotionale Modalitäten der Filmrezeption." *Audiovisuelle Emotionen. Emotionsdarstellung und Emotionsvermittlung durch audiovisuelle Medienangebote.* Ed. Jens Eder, and Kathrin Fahlenbrach. Köln: Halem, 2007. 218-237.

The Fountain. Dir. Darren Aronofsky. Perf. Hugh Jackman and Rachel Weisz. Warner Bros., 2006.

Winko, Simone. "Über Regeln emotionaler Bedeutung in und von literarischen Texten. *Regeln der Bedeutung. Zur Theorie der Bedeutung literarischer Texte.* Ed. Fotis Jannidis, et al. Berlin: de Gruyter, 2003. 329-348.

Wulff, Hans J. "Affektivität als Element der Filmrezeption oder im Kino gewesen, geweint (gelacht, gegruselt...)—wie es sich gehört!" *Mit allen Sinnen. Gefühl und Empfindung im Kino.* Ed. Susanne Marschall and Fabienne Liptay. Marburg: Schüren, 2006. 17-31.

FREDERIKE OFFIZIER

Death of the Other: Dying, Alterity, and Appropriation

> Madame, all stories, if continued far enough, end in death, and he is no true storyteller who would keep that from you. (Hemingway, *Death in the Afternoon*)

Death and dying are undoubtedly considered morbid topics, and the prolonged occupation with them is deemed "unhealthy" in the literal sense of the Latin word.[1] Today even prolonged mourning is regarded as shameful and morbid: "it is a sign for mental instability or bad manner" (Ariés 1974: 90). But that was not always the case. Philipp Ariés shows in his historical studies *Western Attitudes toward Death* (1974) and *The Hour of Our Death* (1981) that within the last century the attitudes toward death and dying have changed at an unprecedented velocity. In the 20th century dying turned into a taboo that was hidden from the dying person and eventually interdicted in public entirely.[2] This "brutal revolution" (1974: 85), as he calls the transition that altered the attitude toward death and dying, is believed to have started in the United States where the culture of life had replaced the fear of death (Farrell 5). Not surprisingly then, contemporary culture is marked by the self-made life and body project and the denial of death (cf. Becker). These changes were influenced by developments in medical knowledge, spiritual belief, and living conditions, and led to "modern dying [being] a paradox: it is difficult, expensive, and prolonged but at the same time invisible" (Coulehan 561).

However, "[s]hown the door by society, death is coming back in through the window, and it is returning just as quickly as it disappeared" (Ariés 1981, 560). In the last decades dying has re-entered public discourse and is increasingly placed on political agendas all over the world. To speak about the invisibility of death and dying in the 20th century seems counter-intuitive. It is not only a century of major wars and brutal genocides, the possibilities of photo and camera have brought the horrors of mass dying closer to (non-afflicted) people as ever before. But this paper is not concerned with mass dying. It is the representation of the individual coming to an end that reveals the human complexities beyond biological death of a body.

---

1   Lat. morbidus: diseased, unhealthy
2   Geoffrey Gorer compared in his article "The Pornography of Death" the attitude toward death to the Victorian attitude toward sex (cited in Ariés 1974: 92). In the United States, in contrast to continental Europe, this drastic exclusion from public space did not affect traditions of burial and post-mortem treatment. It evolved into an elaborate and often extravagant performance with a booming post-mortem industry (cf. Mitford).

The fascination of the great Other, the ultimate unknown has drawn artists of all times and cultures into the gravitational space of what today is considered morbid, unhealthy, ugly, and unaesthetic. Death and dying are one of the most consistently aestheticized human "experiences." From the biblical representations of Christ's death on the cross, Hector's death on the battlefield, to the beautification of death in Sentimentalism and Emily Dickinson's analytic poems, representations of dying exemplify the politics of aesthetics as well as the changing "realities" of passing. What all of them have in common is that dying has seldom been perceived or represented as a purely "natural" event without greater implications.

As a purely physiological process dying is meaningless. Nonetheless, most frequently dying is the host of a whole array of meanings, which are not instilled into nothingness but rather "recognized" in the embodiment of the process. Only by the enactment of pain, fear, suffering, panic, or even content and hope is meaning created within a cultural context, and almost exclusively by others. In referring to Judith Butler's theory of performativity I suggest that the process of dying relies on a cultural narrative that makes the performance of dying not only understandable but essentially creates it. Though the physicality of passing is governed by material decay, it is the performativity of the dying body that mitigates the meaning of the process. As "bodies can be conceived as dying but persons cannot" (Cassell 1973: 171), cultural narratives provide the means to understand and represent the dying of a person.

Alan Warren Friedman suggests, "death is always fictional" (3), however, I wish to broaden this allegation because also *dying* is constructed and inevitably fictional. In fact, the reality of the process is constituted and exists only by virtue of narratives because the story of dying that is told after the death of a person cannot escape its narrativization; and, furthermore, the process of dying especially in its latter stage can only be perceived based on cultural narratives that provide the intelligibility of the process. In literary dying scenes the artistic expression and imagination draws attention to the problems and pitfalls in presenting the end of life. Moving toward the limits of representability the narratives of dying have to reveal their entanglement in discourse, while providing a meaningful "de-Composition" of the fictive character. Arriving at the limits of representation writing challenges and trespasses those limits making them perceptible, that is, legible.

Literary renderings therefore often stress the eternal Otherness of dying, though philosophically and spiritually one's own death/dying is supposed to be the most truthful and real moment in a person's life, its closure. Popular notions of a greater understanding of life are bequeathed in the cultural imagery of "life flashing by," which is based on this construction.[3] Memoirs and obitu-

---

[3] In Christian tradition the relation of individual biography and dying emerged around the same time as the *ars moriendi*. "It was thought that each person's entire life

aries, as summaries of the deceased's life, reveal a similar notion of postmortem judgment, especially regarding persons of public interest. Death is thus, as Michel Foucault puts it, "the absolute point of view over life and opening [...] on its truth" (1994: 155).[4] As implicit in the understanding of dying as the moment of retrospection, the notion of conclusion is often interlaced with the belief in a greater awareness of oneself in dying. The iconic value of last words uttered on the deathbed illustrates this conceptualization of the final moments leading to revelation: a more profound understanding of life. Up until today last words represent the fictitious possibility of "dying a linguistically meaningful death" (Fuss 877).

Death is in Heidegger's words one's "ownmost" (68) not only possibility but also experience. It is the "one" which is unknowable and unexperienceable by a third person. The prioritization of the self in dying separated from the experience of the other's death, as Alphonso Lingis describes the most common perspective of philosophy, seems to obliterate that dying is primarily a relational process of othering/otherness: it is the encounter with the Other in all its different garments. It is important to recognize this and look at dying as more than the *memento mori*, which dominates the imagery and terminology of death and dying in the Humanities. The death of the Other is far more than merely a reminder of one's own mortality, because in dying Self and Other become intricately linked in the negotiation of meaning, understanding, and perceiving.

In this paper I will therefore focus on four dimensions that determine this Self and Other relation. First I will give a brief historical overview of the practice of and relation to death and dying to show in what ways the perspective of the death of the Other has dominated cultural attitudes. I will then turn to the perspective of the Other as decisive for the knowledge and understanding of dying. In "The Self as Other" I will focus on the relation between Self and Body to emphasize that also one's own dying is caught in the inevitable sociality of dying. In concluding I will offer a fourth dimension of the "death of the Other." It is the appropriation and obliteration of Otherness through the normative power of biomedical discourse, or rather through the post-modern turn to quantifiable analytics and measurable effects. In this context the unknowability and unrepresentability of dying is oppressed in favor of scientific factual discourse.

---

    flashed before his eyes at the moment of death. It was also believed that his attitude at that moment would give his biography its final meaning, its conclusion" (Ariés 1974: 38).

4   Foucault is originally referring to the double meaning of "opening" as he is focused on the constitution of knowledge of life through the practice of autopsies.

From *mort moi* to *mort toi*

Ariés asserts that until the 18th century persons were primarily concerned with their own death, "la mort de soi." From then on death and dying became increasingly marked by intense beautification and dramatization. People became "less concerned with [their] own death than with *la mort de toi*, the death of the other person, whose loss and memory inspired in the nineteenth and twentieth centuries the new cult of tombs and cemeteries and the romantic, rhetorical treatment of death" (Ariés 56).

But Romantic writing was not only fascinated with the life to death transition, it increasingly interlaced deathbed scenes with expressions of mourning. The deathbed scene of Little Eve in Harriet Beecher Stowe's *Uncle Tom's Cabin* is one of the most famous and epitomizing literary renderings in the 19th century in US American Literature. The beautiful death of Sentimentalism does not even leave an "imprint [on Eve's face], —only a high and almost sublime expression, —the over shadowing presence of spiritual natures, the dawning of immortal life in that childish soul" (Beecher Stowe 256). Eve's passing turns into a spectacle of spiritual enlightenment for the witnesses. Nonetheless, her father moans, how terrible the dying is mirroring the shift from "mort moi" to "la mort de toi" (Ariés 68).

This fascination with death and dying—its aesthetization, beautification, and eroticization—is not to be confused with familiarity and acceptance, much less with a stable understanding. Rather the obsession with the "coming to an end" of a person, as e.g. in the 19th century seems to parallel a destabilization of beliefs and concerns regarding death and dying. While the rise of science had diminished the belief in the religious narrative of the beyond as heaven or hell, modes of representation altered radically in the wake of Romanticism and rise of Sentimentalism. The excessive beautification of and fascination with death saturates the literature of the century with subtle distinctions. The 19th century is often referred to as the "morbid century." This denomination is emblematic for the shift in the meaning of morbidity. Many critics stress the familiarity with death during that time, however, Castronovo points out that "for cultures that fear death [...] necrophilia promotes fascination with and helps tame an unknown terror" (5). Instead of familiarization it is thus growing uncertainty that seem to spur the cultural production of that time. The advances in medical knowledge strengthened "the conception of death as disease" (Farell 60), which could be mastered and eventually eradicated. Thus, the death of the Other was exceedingly the cause for sorrow and unease as in Mark Twain's "Heaven or Hell," where "dissimulation has become the rule" (Ariés 1981: 562). The short story centers around a mother and a daughter, who are both sick and dying, and the chain of lies between them, their doctor, and the two care-giving aunts. The final moments of dying are nonetheless marked by a peaceful vision of the beyond. So while the religious and cosmological perspective on dying maintained a meaningfulness of the physicality of dying, by the end of the 19th century the splendid beyond and the meaning of suffering were increasingly replaced by tropes of annihilation and meaninglessness.

A prime example of such a publication is *The Gates Ajar* (1868)[5] by Elizabeth Stuart Phelps. It is a mourner's manual, which describes a paradisiacal beyond "complete with hospital for sick souls who receive the ministration of spirit doctors" (Jackson 63). This consolation literature of "openly fictionalized and avowedly factual accounts of deathbed scenes and celestial communications crowded the bookstalls in the decades before and after the Civil War" (Douglas 50). However, it was not considered morbid.[6]

While the concern with the Other's death remained, it has yet attained different form. Today, this concern for the Other's death is not only a cultural attitude but in many cases a legal procedure. The twentieth and twenty-first-century are marked by the complete medicalization and legalization of death. The possibilities and intents to cure transformed the dying subject into a sick person and led to the practice of withholding the fatal condition from the patient until the very end.[7] The dying individual, once the subject of his or her last rite of passage turned into the object of medical routine detracted of any former social ritual. Furthermore, the dying were "sanitized" out of the public space displaced into hospitals, palliative care units, hospices, and care facilities as the achievements of medical research have not only prolonged life but have extended the process of dying. Dying has turned from a natural into a rather "technical phenomenon obtained by a cessation of care" (Ariés 1974: 88). Since "[t]oday people characteristically die at an age when their physical, social, and mental powers are at an ebb, or even absent" (Blauner 194) the authority over the dying is distributed between the doctors, bioethics and legal committees, the family or legal guardian, and the individual if he or she has in advance prepared with a "living will," the modern addition to the testament. The predominant perspective on the process of dying is thus decisively marked by Otherness. Not only is it medical personal that is the "new gatekeeper" of death and the decisive element of when dying starts and ends, increasingly death has become an active decision that lies beyond the control and consciousness of the individual. And this does not only account for sensational

---

5   The book was so successful that in 1883 *Beyond the Gates*, and in 1887 *The Gates Between* were published (excerpt published in Jackson 1977).

6   I would argue that today a similar "genre" has re-emerged with the illness narratives and growing number of mourning literature. It indicates a new paradigm shift, or new degree of uncertainty that is again motivated by the destabilization of a "religious" discourse, that of science. Doctors and western medicine have lost their status of "half-gods in white," and are increasingly challenged by alternative concepts and ethical reproaches.

7   This trend would continue well into the 1980s and is today termed the "regime of silence" (Ariés 1975: 138).

cases of brain death or the use of life prolonging measures. Given that "the average American male now is debilitated for five years before he dies, and the average American female for eight years" (Hardwig 37), care becomes paramount in considering the end of life. Already the at times lengthy anticipation (of sometimes several years) is accompanied by the need for and dependence on other people.

In his memoirs of his mother's death, David Rieff states that "What seemed to her (and rightly) like such a swift and terrible spiral downward afforded those of us around her almost too much time to prepare ourselves for the finality of her passing" (161). On 160 pages he elaborates on the anticipation of dying that is only recognizable as such because of the proleptic knowledge of Susan Sontag's death. Otherwise, the narrative echoes illness narratives, such as Audre Lorde's *Cancer Journals* (1985), which are stories of fighting, possible explanations and cures. However, in the final deathbed scene the feared end was "merciful" (Rieff 163).

> She remained intermittently lucid for another day, though her throat was so abaded that she could barely speak audibly and she was confused. I *feel* she knew I was there but I am not all sure. [...] By Monday afternoon she had left us, though she was still alive. Preterminal, the doctors call it. It was not that she wasn't there or was wholly unconscious; she was neither. But she had gone to a place deep within herself, to some last redoubt of her being, at least as I imagine it. (Rieff 163-164)

This narrative construction of dying exemplifies the central position of the Other as the one that has to "bring the process to an end" once it exceeds the dying's capacities. As witnesses they become the decisive element in bringing the story to a closure, and are the ultimate source of giving meaning to the Other's death: in Sontag's case the merciful death after long suffering.

Self and Other: the Witness

Though the process of dying of the Self is commonly separated from the experience of someone else's dying, I will argue that it is intricately linked to the dying of the Other on multiple levels. It is the only communicable perspective on dying and therefore establishes the ultimate meaning of the process. Furthermore, or at the same time, the Other's death is the basis for the dying to understand their own passing. In that perspective the sense of the "performativity of dying" becomes clear. It demonstrates the intersection of performance and performativity, inscribing a structure of witnessing and staging. This configuration of looking and being looked at—which is necessary to establish the meaning of the process—is constitutive for the understanding of perishing life.

The most obvious relation implied by "the death of the Other" is the dying—witness relation. It is inherent in any representation of dying since the narrativization of the process relies on this perspective for its completion, and is in fact the prerequisite for representation as such. Without the retrospective narrativization the story can never attain meaning because the end point lies beyond the possibilities of self-representation. However, dying is nonetheless a unique and deeply individual process that is, as Heidegger wrote, one's "ownmost non-relational possibility" (294). Despite the implications of authenticity, Heidegger formulates the impossibility to replace someone else in dying (*Vertretbarkeit*) as well as to experience someone else's death and dying as such. As a spectator one is only able to perceive the transition from living body to corpse from the outside, as "we have no way of access to the loss-of-being which the dying man suffers" (Heidegger 282). The story of a passing is thus bound by an outside perspective, by Otherness. This ontological dilemma becomes obvious when looking at narrative constructions of dying.

The difficulties that arise within a narrative configuration of dying reside primarily in the questions of voice and perspective. While first person narrator and character focalization provide an internal view of thoughts and feelings, the scene can never be completed through this perspective. Frequently "the narrative is continued by other narrators after the death" (Stanzel 229). These narrative breaks, both, Stanzel's shift between narrators and Genette's shift of focalization, are symptomatic of dying scenes across time and genres. The "impossibility" of representing dying therefore resides with the perspective of the narration because it has to represent the gap between the dying's and spectator's perspective which are inevitably disparate.

When Toni Morrison describes her heroine's death in *Sula* she renders this divide legible in the spatial construction of the deathbed in contrast to the room. The childhood friend Nel visits the bedridden Sula in her house. While the room is delineated by a semi-permeable boundary (the door), the deathbed designates the last threshold that is not passed. Though present at the deathbed Nel is explicitly staying outside of this confined space of dying. "Nel's finger closed around the brass rail of the bed" (2165) and the experience of this uncrossable divide between living and dying is so intense that "[t]he feeling of the brass was in Nel's mouth" (2165). It is not just a physical boundary of the rail, but an affective border as Morrison transfers the physical feeling on to a sensual experience. The spatial implications reiterate the cultural narrative of dying as an ultimately solitary experience. Furthermore, the image of the affective border points toward the impossibility of experiencing the dying of the Other because the "brass railing" will remain an insurmountable border for the witness. Experiencing someone's dying is inextricably different to the firsthand experience of dying. Though compassion, friendship, and mourning might help to bridge part of this insurmountable divide of Self and Other, "[i]n facing and having to deal now with this absolute, NOTHINGNESS [sic], the dying Other is alone" (Valberg 230).

The inevitably "abortive" outside perspective of the witness nonetheless determines the ultimate meaning of dying. To return to the example of Morrison's *Sula*: in the internally focalized passages of the text, Sula's passing is predominantly represented in positive imagery, which is contrasted to the outside view of her childhood friend Nel and the community. Morrison establishes a narrative of the normal rituals taking place when someone dies in the fictive community, which serves as a comparative blueprint for Sula's dying. Most of these typical features of the representation of dying seem to indicate a "bad death," which the reader learns exclusively through Nel's comments. At first glance it is a de-idealized portrait of dying: Sula has no visitors, though it was common in the community of the Bottom to take care of each other, and she has not even a "wallet, [and] no change purse" (2163). Not surprisingly, Sula's rite of passage falls short of what was common in the Bottom. Nonetheless Sula was happy in her solitariness in dying as she fares with a smile. However, it is not only the circumstances of her death that are misread by her friend, but also retrospectively by the community.

For the outer world that is left "reading the corpse," her smile would have been the ultimate "trace" of a peaceful death—the potential proof of a cultural narrative "acting" upon the body. But upon the discovery of the corpse, the cypher of the body is read quite differently: "[H]e knew she was dead right away not because her eyes were open but because her mouth was open. It looked to him like a giant yawn that she never got to finish" (2179). This reading of the corpse overemphasizes the impossibility of communicating dying. The "witness" merely discovers "the body [that] was still lying in Eva's bed gazing at the ceiling trying to complete the yawn" (2179). The smile, which is essential for the reader's understanding of Sula's dying, comes to epitomize the discrepancy between different perspectives representing merely a reading of the body. But Sula's dying is further appropriated: "it was a clear sign of the mystery of God's ways, His mighty thumb having been seen on her [Sula's] throat" (2169). Though none of the people were present and nobody but the white mortuary workers could have seen Sula's throat, the Bottom established their own narrative of Sula's process of dying. In the collective memory Sula's body performs the meaning the townspeople read into her death: God took her life to relief them. Sula's death is thus appropriated and the ultimate and persistent meaning comes from without.

The perspective of the witness is decisive on multiple levels and not only functions to guarantee the subsequent representation and commemoration in form of a narrative. The witness of a process of dying does not only interpret the facts of the death but the enactment and embodiment of the entire process. If not present during the process, this practice is often conducted retrospectively, as e.g. with autopsies and the determination of the cause of death. The importance of such narratives is not only obvious in criminal cases but also in e.g. mundane everyday news items, which interlace the announcement of death frequently with "instantly dead," "tortured to death," "after long suffering."

The proximity of Butler's theory to theatrical performance was one of the heavily criticized aspects. Statements such as "one does one's body" (Butler 1988: 521) made gender practices appear as a deliberate choice and threatened to diminish them to interchangeable and somehow intentionally artificial acts. Though Butler distanced her writing in *Bodies that Matter* from explicit references to theatricality, I would like to suggest that the notion of the theatrical performance is (though problematic) increasingly important for the understanding of dying.[8]

The perspective of dying as performance, without which the process would remain inaccessible and illegible, is essential for the communication and creation of meaning. In dying the bodily process becomes an act—though not governed by a conscious controlling mind—in that it is staged and closely observed (by doctors, friends, and family—if present—and the self). Though the deteriorating body thwarts any intentionality of the subject, the body is never to itself, but always and already in society, it is always on display, "impressed upon by others, impinging upon them as well" (Butler 2004: 27). As such it relies on similar structures as staged theatrical performances of spectator and actor in which the interaction of actors and audience constitute the performance (Fischer-Lichte, 47). Performativity in its double-meaning of "'dramatic' and 'non-referential'" (Butler 1988: 522) emphasizes a "being in the world" that relies in all of its aspects—public and private life—on a dialectic structure between the individual and the society. Dying can thus not be absolved from the relation to the Other.

Performativity is essentially based on communication to produce its effect, it requires a second person similar to Austin's interlocutor.[9] Similarly dying requires such a space. In focusing on the legitimacy and intelligibility of performance Andrew Parker and Eve Kosofsky Sedgwick describe this as a "space of encounter" (9) where the position of the witness is of crucial importance. In other words, if my performance is not recognized as such, it fails. With "recognizing" I do not refer to a general intelligibility of my act, but rather the recognition of its effect. This is not to say that people would not die without a witness, but that the "reading of the witness" is essential for the meaning of the performance. "Although we struggle for rights over our own bodies, the very bodies for which we struggle are not quite ever only our own.

---

8   I am aware that "the stretch between theatrical and deconstructive meanings of 'performative' seems to span to polarities of, at either extreme, the *extroversion* of the actor, the *introversion* of the signifier" (Parker/Sedgwick 2). Nonetheless, I think that both understandings are crucial for the approach of performativity since also a suppression of acts are in my understanding a form of extroversion. However, my argument will largely follow the deconstructive meaning of performativity.

9   In his study of performative utterances Austin asserts, "it is very commonly necessary that either the speaker himself or other persons should *also* perform certain *other* actions, whether ‚physical' or mental actions or even acts of uttering further words." (8) In regard to the communicative aspect of performativity, however, the "second person" is not to be understood as a physical person, though in many cases it is, but rather as a space of negotiation.

The body has its invariably public dimension. Constituted as a social phenomenon in the public sphere, my body is and is not mine" (Butler 2004: 26). And this is especially true for narratives of the process of dying. It can never be fully nor completely mine, in that it requires a watching or witnessing, a reading and accepting or refusing to accept that which it means.

In the readings of the body in dying the boundary of performativity and performance dissolves easily between constitutive constraint and willed participation. Even in the moments of unwilled and physically inscribed performativity we encounter a mode of staging and/or hiding. What is put on stage, or rather revealed to the outside, even if not intentionally produced by the subject plays a fundamental role for the comprehension of the corporeality of dying materiality. When Butler writes that "the *appearance of substance* [sic] is precisely that, a constructed identity, a performative accomplishment which the mundane social audience, including the actors themselves, come to believe and to perform in the mode of belief" (1988: 520), it is the appearance which is the precondition for a performative accomplishment. In that sense a materiality that "bears meaning" (Butler 1988: 521) can only bear it if it is looked upon.

However, the performativity of dying does not only imply the appropriation of dying by the Other but extends toward the perspective of the Self. Since the bodily performance is intrinsic to individual reality, dying bares the structure of spectacle, not only for the Other but also for the Self. Given the perpetual futurity of death, anticipation and comparative conceptions bound by previously established narratives influence the perception of the materiality in dying. As in Elizabeth Bronfen's analysis of Hodler's paintings of the dying Valentine Godé-Darel, the gaze at the body is a "self-portrait" (48) rather than a reality that exists independently and outside the self. This does not only apply to the relation of artist and object, but also to the "conventional" relation of spectator and spectacle, which structurally equals that of self and body.

Self as Other

Death is not only un-experienceable for the Other but also for the Self. In contrast to Heidegger, Levinas asserts that death is "an event in relation to which the subject is no longer subject" (1987: 70). In resorting to Epicurus famous sentence "If you are, death is not; if death is you are not" (*Letter to Menoeceus*, qtd. in Levinas 1987: 71), Levinas questions the very possibility of the experience of death and dying. Since death marks the complete dissolution of the experiencing subject, the end of dying remains in an "eternal futurity" (1987: 71) for the dying and is in that sense not only "unknown but unknowable, refractory to all light" (1987: 75) remaining eternally Other.

The relation to one's own death is therefore that to "a future that never arrives" (Cohen 32) and remains caught in the anticipation of an event that is unknown, or rather imaginary. Even though the futurity of death generally refers to the last moments of the process of dying, I would suggest that the knowledge of impending death, "the notion of dying soon," entails the same characteristics as the notion of "not yet" referring to death. Since the time of dying is "a temporality of infinite delay, patience, senescence or difference" (Critchley 75) the individual can never be absolutely sure of its own coming to an end.

If we are not able to experience our own death, the only relation to death that is possible is the death of the Other, and following that logic, death only exists for and through the Other (cf. Suglia 53). Theoretically it is only in the others that have ceased to exist in my world, that I know what my death means and in that sense indeed "[t]he ultimate meaning of death comes to the self from the other's mortality not its own" (Cohen 27). This is not reducible to a pure *memento mori* for the survivor, but has to be understood in a more intricate way of "meaning making." Though I do not agree with Levinas' ethical claim of the priority of the Other's mortality over mine,[10] the notion of the Other in dying has important implications for the understanding and experience of the process. It establishes the narratives of dying that infiltrate the individual process of anticipation, which is the determinative characteristic of dying.

In *For Whom the Bell Tolls*, one of the most famous dying scenes of American literature shows the Hemingwayan hero in his final meditations. Tracing the thoughts of the hero in pain reveals the performative force within the process of dying, which is bound by previously established narratives. The pain-ridden mind fluctuates between explanations for his corporeality and thoughts of suicide. The undirected rhetoric question "not to misunderstand" suicide shows that Robert Jordan is at the same time alone in his dying and not. By letting the character consider the survivor's perspective, which will ultimately determine the meaning of his death, Hemingway emphasizes the inherently social and performative nature of dying. After the onset of pain the character argues with himself until the very end about the legitimacy of suicide in his situation. However, it is not suicide only as a theoretical and detached concept, but suicide as "the business that my father did" (488) that increases his disregard and lets him hold out and wait for death. The Other's death in form of personal experience or internalized discourse is thus present in the Self, while being absent.

Since the perspective of dying is marked by anticipation and eternal futurity the body becomes an enigmatic sign for the self as well. With "audience or spectator" constellation I therefore wish to include the subject itself, which turns into the "compulsory witness" (Parker/Sedwick) of its own body. The individual is indeed passive, in the sense that it does not actively perform,

---

10   "In that relation with the face, in a direct relation with the death of the other, you probably discover that the death of the other has priority over yours, and over your life" (Levinas 1995: 164).

however, in "decoding" the body it is incredibly active. The body becomes stage and actor at the same time, "reducing" the subject to the role of the witness of its own body in dying.

In Hemingway the reading and interpreting of the wound and its symptoms by the dying hero himself becomes increasingly scientific as the scene progresses. Initially free of pain Robert Jordan gives a "detached" and objective self-diagnosis that appears factual, almost as if preformed from an outside perspective. This mode of expression is also maintained during the reading of pain: "What I think is you've got an internal hemorrhage there from where that thigh bone's cut around inside. [...] That makes the swelling and that's what weakens you and makes you start to pass" (489). This last reading of the body, following the contemplation of suicide, represents a rational and diagnostic mind trying to explain to the suffering self the factual cause of his corporeal pain. The narrative structure of witnessing and explaining evokes a "factual" materiality of the body rendering legible the intangible bodily experience without showing the effect on body and mind at the same time.

However, the seemingly causal explanation of Robert Jordan's suffering remains caught up in the failure of representation. By the division of feeling and fact Hemingway does not only separate body and self, but reveals in the description the limitation of this endeavor. Representing only the physical cause and detached from it the mental effect the description opens a gap which is "the moment when the story must falter," as Butler would suggest. While the "factual" description of the body seems to circumvent the *pathos* of a suffering hero, the inherent interconnectedness to the meaning of pain and suffering indicates the impossibility of a "pure" or "natural" perception of the dying body in the case of Robert Jordan. In essence the diagnostic style of the explanation attempts to narratively "tame" the uncontrollable pain.

Like Robert Jordan, Sula observes her body attentively during her suffering. At the very end of the scene Morrison grants Sula the privilege of last words from beyond the grave, which end with "[w]ell, I'll be damned,' she thought, 'it didn't even hurt. Wait'll I tell Nel'" (2168). The employment of the narrative break, which is unique within the novel, is the only way for Morrison to represent the finality of dying from the perspective of the character. The use of the voice "from beyond" permits Sula's death to be tellable and legible, but most importantly illustrates the limits of the communicability of dying. Sula's final wish to "tell Nel" converges the impossibility to completely experience the dying of the other, while granting the dying the possibility of the ontologically impossible: the experience of her own death. Sula turns into a "native informant" only for the privileged position of the reader, for the actual communication of her experiences are not represented within the novel. The comparison of expectation and experience by the dead character and the conclusive desire to communicate this experience indicate the limits of understanding and representing a process of dying outside of a performative matrix. Furthermore, the statement from beyond emphasizes the relationality of the *experience* of dying. By relating Sula's dying to an internal character expectation, Morrison reveals that even Sula herself can only read the performance of her dying along the lines of a previously established narrative.

The scene reveals that the dying self does not read her bodily performance naïvely, but anticipates the course of the performance, in this case the increase of pain. Sula *expects* her dying to follow a certain path that she imagines or knows dying as. The materiality of the body does not reveal a mere natural and unique process, but instead a bodily performance that is put in relation to a cultural narrative. The materiality of the body is as Butler puts it, not perceivable in its pre-discursive and thus meaningless existence.

Dying, as Heidegger asserted, is an activity one undertakes alone. That means that there should not be anything but the "pure/true" experience of the dying. In contrast, Morrison allows Sula to articulate expectations toward her own dying, for example the pain she anticipates. But more explicitly, Morrison formulates Sula's expectations for her mental self during the process of dying. The protagonist ponders about her prospects:

> [S]he might draw her legs up to her chest, close her eyes, put the thumb in her mouth. [...] [And] float over and down the tunnels, just missing the dark walls, down, down until she met a rain scent and would know the water was near, and she would curl into its heavy softness and it would envelope her, carry her, and wash her tired flesh always. Always. [...] Who was it that had promised her a sleep of water always? (2168)

In this proleptic reflection Morrison creates a complex imagery that reiterates the return to a fetal existence. Sula performatively—in the sense of a cultural script and a bodily performance—returns to a fetal state, the room figuring as the womb that holds her, a position that reflects vulnerability as well as primary trust. Though Sula does not remember who it was that introduced her to this idea, Morrison clearly reveals the dependence on a cultural narrative concerning the representation and the understanding of the process of dying. For the reader Morrison resolves the riddle of "always" in a later meditation of Shadrack. "He had said 'always,' so she would not have to be afraid of the change—the falling away of skin, the drip and slide of blood, and the exposure of bone underneath [...] to convince her of permanency" (2171). Morrison thus shows how even the self-perception or reading of one's own body relies on a cultural narrative, and by doing so reveals the inevitability of dying as performance. The text therefore demonstrates the failure of her representation of the human in dying that has to render the gap between the perspective of the dying and the perspective of the Other. Only by the use of the cultural narrative is Morrison able to write an intelligible process of dying as a meaningful event that is not tied exclusively to a factual physicality but rather to a prior set of established meanings. In dying the Self thus encounters its own body as Other, as a readable text.

Appropriating the Other

Dying has attained a central place in many cultures and mythologies and is often associated with a greater understanding, a deeper truth, which leads the religious into eternity and the existentialist to nothingness. Today in the age of a "religion of science" the technological and medical advances have forced the abjected end of life back into conversation, which is led primarily by professionals. Denied, hidden and silenced in the public, the process of dying is in so much need of professional attention and management, that it required further specialization of palliative care, hospice care, psychological and social care. To establish dying as Other might seem banal at first sight. However, today dying is an institutionalized and technological process that is primarily governed by the biomedical discourse, which tends to obliterate this inherent Otherness of their object of study.

When medical discourse usurped the authority over the process of dying death was treated as a curable disease though it was obviously inevitable. Letting someone die without treating the "last" infection was simply not acceptable in the master narrative of the medically controllable body and life. This "new ritual" of the deathbed exemplifies the ruthless appropriation of the Other by science which changed and challenged the relation to the body and life. Margaret Edson's Play *Wit* (1999) traces the experience of the main protagonist Vivian Bearing from the diagnosis of stage IV ovarian cancer through the treatment and subsequent death. While the character consistently stresses her identity as "a professor of seventeenth-century poetry, specializing in the Holy Sonnets of John Donne" (Edson 1) her life becomes quickly a matter of medical history: "J: Are your parents living? V: No. J How and when did they die? [...] Cancer? [...] Well, that about does it for your life history. V: Yes, that's all there is to my life story. J: Now I'm going to ask you about your past medical history" (Edson 14). The interview continues over several pages representing the onset of a medical treatment in which the person is lost in the hospital routine during her fight against death, though denominationally she fights cancer. When Vivian starts to fail again and again as a consequence of the aggressive chemotherapy, she is further treated until the "do not resuscitate order" finally saves her from another reanimation and further prolongation of life. Besides the cruelties of medical practice, the play epitomizes the appropriation of bodily processes by a discourse that claims supreme authority and benevolence. For the medical personal of the play the character is rather an object of research. More importantly, the language used by the doctors labels and categorizes the different processes of Vivian's physical decline, diminishing the experience of dying to dissected medical problems, dehumanizing her until she becomes "code blue, room 707" (Edson 54). In a broader perspective:

> [T]he material body is remade through a language that denies itself, [...] couched in empirical discourse in order to present as natural and inevitable what are in fact powerfully motivated narratives of the body, its value, and its place within the human community. (Miller 33)

This violent appropriation of the experience of dying has been significantly challenged since the 1980s. The recognition of the inaptitude of curative medicine to deal appropriately with the process of dying has led to a whole field of research. Thanatology is an "interdisciplinary approach that combines medical science, psychology, social science, nursing, and social work, studying the dying as well as the bereaved with the aim of ensuring 'proper care'" (Rhodes/Vedder 3).

Though these concepts of the dying experience represent important findings regarding the care of patients, they also raise various difficulties. The entire field of study is based on the prerequisite of awareness in dying and is primarily focused on terminally ill patients. But "dying facing one's own death in a matter of hours, days, or weeks is neither a human experience confined to illness nor a simple journey of decline and open awareness" (Kellehear 389). Moreover, the translation of suffering into categories does not only risk to dissolve the experience in clinical and academic terminology, dying as a subject seems far too diverse to be encompassed by empirical studies. A field of research that produces stages, phases, and categories represents the process of dying as a predictable and controllable process that can, with the proper measures, follow a culturally prescribed course. A development that fits almost too neatly into the contemporary notion that "too evident sorrow does not inspire pity but repugnance" (Ariés 1974: 90). Moreover, this field of study relies mainly on "observing and interviewing thousands of terminally ill patients" (Rhodes/Vedder 71). The narratives that serve as the most important tool of "learning from the dying" are conducted in anticipation of the terminal stage while the end of the process remains restricted to the interpretation of the spectacle of dying. It is thus the researcher's perspective that has to be kept in mind when reading those interpretations. The "place of interest" (Spivak 279), which should always be considered in the writing or thinking the Other, is therefore the determining factor in the understanding of the entirety of the process. The images and beliefs that are tied to this anticipation thus largely rely on cultural narratives, evermore so since the exposure to death has diminished radically in our day and age.

The diagnosis of a terminal disease is not only a "death sentence" to most patients but also the onset of a new identity and new rules of conduct that the dying person is expected to enact. The increasing efforts to provide an "orderly" framework for the dying seems exceedingly necessary as the lack of ritual in dying seems to be one of the primary sources of suffering (Wouters). However, these attempts to create new rituals not only fail to "convince as authentic" (Wouters 3), moreover they create "new" normative definitions. The trope of "becoming-self" in dying for example stresses a shift of attention from the body to the inner self, leading to comprehensive categories in the practice of nursing, such as "the transcending-self, the becoming-self, and the reconciling-self, along with lower order process patterns of the agonizing-self, the relinquishing-self, and the repressing-self" (Dobratz 138). The clear categorization of preferable and abnegated behavior in dying, though established for therapeutic and benevolent reasons, represents a further delimitation to the dying, who is then not only expected to fight a disease at whatever costs, but to conform to societal expectations and to enact them accordingly.

Furthermore, the generation most actively changing and challenging the practice and understanding of dying—the babyboomers slowly reaching old age—seems, more so than earlier generations, committed to the imperatives of control and the superiority of conscious decisions, and calculability. The medical and technical possibilities, which allow us to enhance and prolong life, and the legalization of physician assisted suicide in single states of the U.S. marks a new era of appropriating death. It is the epitaph of a culture that deems the body a possession, a kind of vehicle that is controllable in every situation. The practice thus does not only obliterate otherness but threatens to eradicate it almost entirely.

Nowadays the instability of the conceptualization of dying is especially prevalent since modern medical technology allows us to modify and substitute physical processes. Suffering and the question of what is humane are thereby exceedingly important and decisive for the procuring of "adequate" treatment. What is at stake when considering the deteriorating body becomes especially evident in looking at current conceptions of good and bad death, especially in regard to dying with dignity, which is centered on "specifically [...] the suffering of the body, and the moral and spiritual problems it creates" (May 14). Today, regression and suffering in dying is viewed as degrading and dehumanizing as heated public and legislative discussions reveal. Even within the medical community perspectives drift apart and are expressive in the distinction between "Hippocratic Medicine" and "New Medicine" (Colbert). While the former restrict their intervention to alleviation and the withdrawal of life prolonging measures, the latter support physician assisted suicide based on the argument of unnecessary and inhumane suffering preceding death. In that sense the understanding that "although the physicality of death destroys us, the idea of death saves us" (Yalom 33) attains new meaning. While living, the recognition of one's mortality leads to living a more fulfilled life, in dying though, death becomes the safety net in the abyss of dehumanization.

Medical discourse is not a purely descriptive entity, but must also be perceived as a powerful performative force in regard to the understanding of normal and abject bodies. Bodily "symptoms" are perceived as enigmatic, which enhances "the notion of bodies as (volatile) text" (Miller 36). But since "there is no reference to a pure body which is not at the same time a further formation of that body" (Butler 1993: 10), these signs are always to be understood as non-referential in the sense that they establish and evoke a "phantasmatic identification" (Butler 1993: 93) between signifier and signified. This is not to indicate that those diseases, physical or mental illness, or certain symptoms are not indicative and "real." However, the cultural meaning with which they are imbued is neither stable nor purely factual in relation to the signs. In that sense corporeality has to be recognized "not as site or surface, but as a process of materialization that stabilizes over time to produce the effect of boundary, fixity and surface we call matter" (Butler 1993: 9). In this sense the body is never quite "our own" as it depends on its legibility within a sign system, it is scripted and represents a "readable narrative" (Klaver 663).

As asserted throughout the centuries, we start to die in the moment we are born because "Dasein is dying as long as it exists" (Heidegger 295). Hence, the process of dying as a defined stage in life is a concept, a fiction designating a deteriorating body, mind, or will to live. This assertion of dying as construct is not meant to advocate the dissolution of existing frameworks of dying by simply indicating their potentially oppressive nature based on prevailing power structures. Instead, it demonstrates that performative constructions are urgently needed as a source of stability and meaning for the individual, and that a cultural critique is essential as a counterbalance to appropriation of dying by the biomedical discourse.

Works Cited

Ariés, Philippe. *The Hour of Our Death*. Trans. Helen Weaver. New York: Vintage Books, 1981.

---. *Western Attitudes Toward Death: from the Middle Ages to the Present*. Trans. Patricia M. Ranum. Baltimore: John Hopkins UP, 1974.

Austin, J.L. *How to Do Things with Words: the William James Lectures delivered at Harvard University*. Oxford: Oxford at the Clarendon Press, 1955.

Becker, Ernest. *The Denial of Death*. 1973. New York: Free Press Paperback, 1997.

Beecher Stowe, Harriet. *Uncle Tom's Cabin*. Ed. Elizabeth Ammons. *Uncle Tom's Cabin: Authoritative Text, Background and Context, Criticism*. New York: Norton and Company, 1994.

Blauner, Robert. "Death and Social Struture." *Passing: The Vision of Death in America*. Ed. Charles O. Jackson. Connecticut: Greenwood Press, 1977. 174-209.

Bronfen, Elisabeth. *Over Her Dead Body: Death, Femininity and the Aesthetic*. Manchester: Manchester UP, 1992.

Butler, Judith. *Precarious Life: The Power of Mourning and Violence*. London, New York: Verso, 2004.

---. *Bodies that Matter: on the Discursive Limits of "Sex"*. New York: Routledge, 1993.

---. *Gender Trouble: Feminism and the Subversion of Identity*. 1990. New York and London: Routledge, 1999.

---. "Performative Acts and Gender Constitution: An Essay in Phenomenology and Feminist Theory." *Theatre Journal* 40. 4 (1988): 519-531.

Cassell, Eric J. "Being and Becoming Dead." *Death in American Experience*. Ed. Arien Mack. New York: Schocken Books, 1973. 162-176.

Castronovo, Russ. *Necro Citizenship: Death, Eroticism, and the Public Sphere in the Nineteenth-Century United States*. Durham, London: Duke UP, 2001.

Cohen, Richard A. "Levinas: Thinking Least about Death—Contra Heidegger" *International Journal of Philosophy of Religion* 60.1/3 (2006): 21-39.

Colbert, Marcella. "The Medicalization of Death and Dying." *Life and Learning XIV. Proceedings of the Fourteenth University Faculty for Life Conference*. Ed. Joseph W. Koterski. Washington D.C., 2004. 227-238. Web 20 February 2012.

Critchley, Simon. *Very Little... Almost Nothing: Death, Philosophy, Literature*. New York: Routledge, 1997.

Douglas, Ann. "Heaven our Home: Consolation Literature in the Northern United States, 1830-1880." *Death in America*. Ed. David E. Stannard. Pennsylvania: U of Pennsylvania P, 1975. 49-68.

Edson, Margaret: *Wit*. New York: Faber and Faber, 1999.

Farrell, James J. *Inventing the American Way of Death, 1830-1920*. Philadelphia: Temple UP, 1980.

Fischer-Lichte, Erika. *Ästhetik des Performativen*. Frankfurt am Main: Suhrkamp, 2004.

Foucault, Michel. *Birth of the Clinic: An Archeology of Medical Perception*. Trans. A. M. Sheridan Smith. New York: Vintage Books, 1994.

Friedman, Allen Warren. *Fictional Death and the Modernist Enterprise*. Cambridge, New York: Cambridge UP, 1995.

Fuss, Diana. "Last Words." *ELH* 76.4 (2009): 877-910.

Hardwig, John. "Going to meet Death: The Art of Dying in the Early Part of the Twenty-First Century." *Hastings Center Report* 39.4 (2009): 37-45.

Heidegger, Martin: *Being and Time*. Trans. John Macquarrie, and Edward Robinson. New York, Evanston: Harper and Row Publishers, 1962.

Hemingway, Ernest. *For Whom the Bell Tolls*. 1941. London: Vintage, 2005.
---. *Death in the Afternoon* .1932. New York: Scribner, 1959.
Jackson, Charles O., ed. *Passing: The Vision of Death in America*. Connecticut: Greenwood Press, 1977.
Kellehear, A. "On Dying and Human Suffering." *Palliative Medicine* 23 (2009): 388-397.
Klaver, Elizabeth. "A Mind-Body-Flesh Problem: The Case of Margaret Edson's Wit." *Contemporary Literature* XLV. 4 (2004): 659-682.
Levinas, Emmanuel. *Alterity and Transcendence*. Trans. Michael B Smith. New York: Columbia UP, 1995.
---. *Time and Other*. Trans. Richard A. Cohen. Pittsburgh, Pennsylvania: Duquesne UP, 1987.
Lingis, Alphonso. "To Die with Others." *Diacritics* 30.3 (2000): 106-113.
Lorde, Audre: *The Cancer Journals* .1980. London: Sheba Feminist Publishers, 1985.
May, William F. "The Sacral Power Of Death in Contemporary Experience." *Death in American Experience*. Ed. Arien Mack. New York: Schocken Books, 1973. 96-122.
Miller, Terri Beth. "'Reading' the Body of Terri Schiavo: Inscriptions of Power in Medical and Legal Discourse." *Literature and Medicine* 28.1 (2009): 33-54.
Mitford, Jessica. *The American Way of Death Revisited*. New York: Alfred A. Knopf, 1998.
Morrison, Toni. *Sula*. 1974. *The Norton Anthology of African American Literature*. Eds. Henry Louis Gates, and Nellie Y. McKay. New York: W.W. Norton and Company, 1997. 2098-2180.
Parker, Andrew, and Eve Kosofsky Sedgwick. "Introduction: Performativity and Performance." *Performativity and Performance*. Eds. Andrew Parker, and Eve Kosofsky Sedgwick. New York: Routledge, 1995. 1-18.
Rieff, David. *Swimming in a Sea of Death: A Son's Memoir*. 2008. London: Ganta, 2009.
Rhodes, Colbert, and Clyde B. Vedder. *An Introduction to Thanatology: Death and Dying in American Society*. Springfield: Charles C. Thomas, 1983.
Spivak, Gayatri Ch. "Can the Subaltern Speak?" *Marxism and the Interpretation of Culture*. Eds. Cary Nelson, and Lawrence Grossberg. Urbana, Chicago: Illinois UP, 1988. 271-313.
Stanzel, Franz K. *A Theory of Narrative*. Trans. Charlotte Goedsche. Cambridge, New York: Cambidge UP, 1984.
Suglia, Joseph. "The Communication of the Impossible." *Diacritics*. 31.2 (2001): 49-69.
Valberg, J.J. *Dream, Death, and the Self*. Princeton, Oxford: Princeton UP, 2007.

Wouters, Cas. "The Quest for New Rituals in Dying and Mourning: Changes in the We-I Balance." *Body and Society* 8.1 (2002): 1-27.

Yalom, Irvin. *Staring at the Sun: Overcoming the Terror of Death*. San Francisco: Jossey-Bass, 2008.

STEPHANIE SIEWERT

"As for France, the Nation has Disposed of You": The Penal Colony as Morbid Space and Discourse of Life

> Le florilège du bagne: melant fantasmes, legends et histoire, le bagne survit, certains dissent comme une cicatrice hideuse et indélébile, d'autres comme un témoignage, certes peu glorieux, d'un siècle de l'histoire sociale de la France. (Pierre Dufour, *Les bagnes de Guyane*, 2006)

A discussion of the history and legends of European penal colonies of the nineteenth and twentieth centuries leads us inevitably into "[t]he realm of the shadow,"—a sphere that "contains partial differences, similarities, and overlaps" (Redfield 16). This does not only refer to the contradictory narratives of convicts, scientists, military administration, missionaries, or journalists, but also to the distinctions and congruencies with other narratives of those who have experienced social exclusion under colonialism, political exile or leprosy in the colonies. Although these experiences cannot be easily compared in terms of practice and consequence, it still seems valid and crucial to note that certain elements of Western history have been assigned a status of invisibility as their presence has become unbearable, dangerous and threatening for the community at "home". Not only did these conceptions facilitate more radical solutions of banishment, but the practice of deportation into far-off regions continuously reaffirmed the peripheral status of social, political and ethnic groups.

Regarding the discussions of unfree labor in colonial and imperial history, the penal colony is a pivotal figure of (im)mobility which forms part of a cultural transfer that has effected both the Atlantic and Pacific history. In the last ten years there has been a heightened interest in the European penal history overseas which could be ascribed to a turn in the Humanities towards biopolitics and studies on discipline and surveillance. The mediation of the brutal reality of political prisons such as Camp X-Ray at Guantanamo Bay has launched a search for answers and explanations in the structural and ideological code of nineteenth century penal practices (see McClintock; Smith). Despite current efforts to excavate the history and imaginary of the modern prison systems, the penal colonies need further attention. Critics such as Peter Redfield have pointed out that many of these places are not merely absent from the national histories, but also from the collective consciousness. Redfield's investigations on French Guiana reveal that the former colony in the South American territory up to today "remains a remarkably insignificant artifact of the political landscape —rarely noticed by most France, let alone anyone else—as well as one of the least settled regions of the world" (Redfield xiv).[1] Furthermore the history of the *bagnes*[2] has not only been a rather neglected topic in the more prominent historiographical works on the long nineteenth century,[3] but equally presents a lacunae of research in cultural and literary studies, with the exception of more prominent works on single authors such as Franz Kafka, whose text "In the Penal Colony" has been re-visited by postcolonial critics such as Karen Piper or Paul Peters. Consequently it remains crucial to ask how myth and legend, history and representation, overlap, and how these narratives elucidate or rather explore the production of precarious identities and the spaces of their fabrication. This paper investigates the connections of history and figuration in Franz Kafka's "In the Penal Colony" (1914) and Schaffner's film *Papillon* (1973) and the way both text and film stage the trajectory of a nineteenth century metropolitan modernity which was shaped by discourses of civilization and savagery.

In turning to the discursive sites of the displaced lies a certain attempt to destabilize and un-mantle common notions of progressivism, evolutionism and humanism. Those concepts provided the explanatory languages and models to justify "fortified enclosure" in the nineteenth and the first half of the twentieth century, and continue to unfold in our time. I will focus on the complex interconnections of racial, social and moral discourses and a rhetorics of decay which affected certain groups within (European metropolis) and outside (colonies) the establishing European nations. Moreover I am interested in how far these overlappings have relied on perceptions of the island as a peripheral concept, a place reserved for those, whose existence was defined *ex negativo* to the metropolitan identity. I assume that literature and film expose the continual

---

1   More recent works on the penal colony as the comparative essay collection on European penal colonies edited by Mario da Passano (2003 [2001]) have stressed that the penal colonies are still an unattended field of research. Yet, there has been vital and groundbreaking national research on the issue by Jacques-Guy Petit, André Zysberg, Michel Pierre, Michelle Perrot (e.g. 1991) and Pierre Dufour (2006). Similarly in the Anglo-American field by Stephen Toth (2006), Alice Bullard (2000), and Peter Redfield (2000). Additionally scholars have turned to the *petites histoires* of the penal colonies, like Emma Christopher's work (2011), which focuses on the interim years of British penal transportation (between the American independence and the transportation to Australia) when the Westcoast of Africa moved to the center of attention and became a disastrous chapter in British penal politics.
2   The French *bagne* originally referred to the "bathhouse" of the Ottoman Empire and the buildings in which prisoners were housed during the period of hostilities between Mediterranean Europe and the Ottoman Empire (Zysberg, 169). It was furthermore applied to those sentenced to rowing Mediterranean galleys and to performing hard labor in Metropolitan ports (ibid.)
3   One of the most prominent and illuminating exceptions is Hannah Arendt's *Origins of Totalitarianism* (1951) which has placed the practices of banishment at the heart of a system of power and distinction that fostered the totalitarian structures of the concentration camp in the twentieth century.

production of a *space* of deviance to which the *place* of the island and the "insularity" of the colony, builds the analogous structure of Otherness. "Space" is here understood to be the discursively produced *topos* entrenched in (historical) space and time. I depart from the assumption that space either belongs to nature, as a "prehistoric stratum" (Foucault 1980: 146), or delineates a "residential site, or field of expansion of peoples, of a culture, of a language or a state" (Foucault 1980: 149), which in both cases assume space as a given, as either "soil" or "domain" (Foucault 1980: 149).

In the following I will contour the historical background of the French penal colonies before I will turn in more detail to the driving forces behind the establishment of the penal colonies in the nineteenth century due to a politics of distinction distributed in scientific and popular theories of degeneration. I will then move on to the site of exclusion itself, examining the "island colony" as a conception and figuration of Otherness in French penal politics. The last part is devoted to the juxtaposition of figure and figuration in two examples from literature and film.

The Penal Colony in History

Michel Foucault's lesson on the role and development of penal practices from the seventeenth to the twentieth century rather shuns the penal colony as an anachronistic model of the modern penal system, as "a distant form of imprisonment" (Foucault 1979: 279), and thus marks it as a *deviation* from his genealogical narrative of modern penal practices and institutions. Foucault did not only underestimate the historical scope and complexity of the penal colonies. He also did not elaborate on the importance of the penal colony for the imperial efforts and body politic of France and other European countries such as Italy, Germany or Portugal, which all held penal colonies abroad, or were discussing the options of installing penal colonies (see Redfield 2005) due to a certain "colonial envy" (Forster 150). [4]

Among others, historicist Stephen Toth has criticized Foucault's position in *Discipline and Punish* for being "a-historical", and "undifferentiated" (Toth

---

4   Historian Colin Forster has attributed the belated effort of penal colonization to colonial or territorial envy, as France had lost almost all its overseas empire in 1814 and was in desperate search for another. As Forster has cogently argued, a newfound colonial empire based on penal colonization was attractive because it would require a concomitant expansion of the navy for transport, provisioning posts, defense, and management (145). New Caledonia was regarded as "an island in the southwest Pacific adjacent to Australia," (Forster 150) meaning adjacent to the British experience of penal transportation which had pointed the way ahead for French penal administration. As for French Guiana, the neighboring Surinam (then Dutch Guiana) had become a flourishing colony and France followed trail of the Dutch not without admiration, which further fostered the urge to accomplish a similar success for their colonial settlements in French Guiana (Lowenthal 37-38).

xi) since the penal colony did not develop *ex nihilo*. It had its origins in "practices of slavery and forced labor in galleys, mines and public works, and [...] in traditions of exile for political figures, nobles, and other members of fallen elites" (Redfield 54). Indeed, the banishment of political prisoners and vagabonds had been a valid measure in almost every European country from the Middle Ages onward. In sixteenth century Britain, forms of slavery and hard labor were employed as penalties for rogues and vagabonds, as King James I instructed the courts to send the felons to "foreign discoveries or other services beyond the seas" (qtd. in Morgan/Rushton 9). During the French Revolution France deported dissidents to the New World where they worked under conditions of indentured servitude (cf. Toth 1).

Yet these developments entered another phase with colonialism and the imperial race. Peter Redfield has emphasized that "[t]he marriage of both labor and exile in the systematized deportation of large numbers of common criminals to New World settlements marks an extreme twist in the eighteenth and nineteenth century" (54). Whereas the British resented to Australia,[5] France found itself in another situation after the American independence. According to the Napoleonic Code of 1810, deportation for political offenses was legal, however, "a suitable overseas replacement for the former American territory could never be found" (O'Brien 260). Whereas earlier colonial experiments in French Guiana (1760-1800) by Jesuits and French entrepreneurs had proven to be disastrous (cf. Lowenthal), and further attempts in 1854 had officially launched the penal colony in French Guiana, France settled on New Caledonia in the Pacific to be "the only place for hard-labor convicts from continental France" in 1867 (Forster 135). Yet this did not mean that French Guiana was no longer used as a place for deportation. However, the discussion on the establishment of French oversea colonies based on penal labor had reached a second climax *after* the British had send their last ships in 1868 to Australia and was further impelled *despite* earlier settlements and plantations in French Guiana had foreshadowed its failure.

As for the implementation of the penal colony French Guiana in the 1850s, the "internal crisis" culminating in the Revolution of 1848 made former experiences neglectable.[6] In order to prevent further turmoil and to find a via-

---

5   The British model is here mentioned *en passant* not so much out of ignorance for the highly influential and complex history of British penal transportation, but more so driven by the choice of material, and also because France and Germany have often been reduced to their histories of ideas which framed the ideological agenda of the penal transportation (see Tocqueville and Beaumont, but also Kant, Forster, and Herder on the concept of race). Contrary to the British penal settlements in Australia and Van Diemen's Island (today Tasmania) little is known about the "experiments" of France in French Guiana and New Caledonia.

6   Britain did not witness the same upheaval of their ruling class in the second half of the nineteenth century as France or Italy. Its insular geography and concomitant myth of

ble solution for the twelve thousand June Days insurgents, Louis Napoleon abandoned them by emergency decree to the territorial holdings overseas (Toth 1). For France a number of possible locales were discussed including Senegal, Madagascar, the Kerguelen Islands and Algeria, until legislation passed in 1854 to establish French Guiana in the South American territory as the new penal colony (Toth 2).

The vital and often controversial discussions of penal labor abroad and the consequent transportation of large numbers of people to overseas holdings by the British Empire produced what Morgan and Rushton have called the "criminal Atlantic"—a system of knowledge that was as much social as cultural. (4) The adaptation of Paul Gilroy's neologism emphasizes the fact that the people who have been shipped abroad have "joined in a wider culture of the dispossessed and exploited" (Morgan and Rushton 7) and although "[i]t has been rightly asserted that migration across the Atlantic was predominantly an African experience [...] within this larger framework convicts could be included in the history of the compulsory mobility of the unfree organized by many early modern European states." (4-5). Hence deportation was not only a practice of the British Empire and much less bound to the Atlantic, since the Pacific region equally experienced its distinct history of deportation and forms of banishment. In addition different forms of unfree labor were interconnected as e.g. the end of the slave trade had a profound impact on the penal politics and practices of deportation.

Colonization depended on cheap labor in the colonies and the loss of slave labor not only caused fears of economic collapse, but equally posed questions concerning the „double logic" of French and British penal politics to *colonize* and *civilize* with a group of people who had been drawn out of the metropolis precisely for their viciousness. The poor and degenerated, the criminals and rebels, the deviant and the defiant were threatening Metropolitan culture, yet advocats of the penal colonies believed that they could overcome their criminal and wasteful "nature" and be installed to colonize the far off colonies. Moreover, at a safe distance, there was a chance to reintegrate them into the economic process and well-being of the mother country. Through hard labor they would purify their soul and pay off their debt while increasing the domain of the Empire. Accordingly, Peter Redfield has emphasized in his discussion of the island imaginary that the penal colony emerged "within the twin languages of modernity, one economic and one moral. The first is more familiar under names such as *industry*, the second as *civilization*" (Redfield 9).

The French *cité morale* depended on a site of disposal and certain strategies of Othering and exclusion. The insular far-off colonies then figured as a paradoxical space, since it was perceived to be a natural site offering kinesis

---

exceptionalism, included an immunization from social contaminations of the European mainland.

and rehabilitation, yet it also evoked images of wilderness and savagery—the potentiality of revolution believed to be intrinsic to the uncivilized land. Ironically, in the end the project of the penal colony fell prey to the "deathliness" of the climate, an incompetent penal administration and uncontrollable epidemics of e.g. yellow fever, which turned the paradisiacal island into a "purgatory," a "[h]ell of limited duration" (Redfield 103-4).

Although the pastoral idea remained a central focus of nineteenth century reformist penal politics, deportation foremost proved to be a very efficient mechanism by which to quietly eliminate criminals and other unwanted persons. The rising criminality and fear of recidivism further spurred the discourse of "social defense" (Toth 35) and social theories "provided a language for political debate, means of public hygiene and national self-preservation" (Toth 36). In the writings of Alexandre Lacassagne and Gustave Le Bon the idea of rehabilitation was displaced by a concern for the protection of the country. Fearing that the metropolis was at the verge of chaos, their theories assured that the country could only protect itself from the internal threat of criminality by expelling offenders to the "faraway colonies in Africa, Asia, and Oceania where civilization does not yet exist" (Le Bon, qtd. in Toth 35). Daniel Pick has emphasized that theories of degeneration as developed in Europe by Bénédict Augustin Morel, Cesare Lombroso, or Max Nordau "were imbricated with an imperialistic insistence on the racial superiority of the world's colonisers over the colonised, but they also reflected back on European society in deeply unsettling ways" (21). At a moment when the European countries experienced a restructuring of their social and economic order, the inward gaze was infected by a certain ideology and politics of distinction that was also part and parcel of the imperial project. Moreover these ideas were not bound to the intellectual or political elite, but circulated as ideas in (pseudo)scientific writings, sentimental literatures, political pamphlets and economic treatises of the time:

> Indeed social questions involving crime, moral decadence and racial pollution began to intersect more and more insistently around the middle of the century. Between the 1820s and the 1840s a massive new literature had emerged charting the phenomenon of crime in the cities: a plethora of sensational stories fetishised, romanticised and reviled the criminal mysteries of a Paris, a Naples, London. Dangerous classes and dangerous races multiplied in literature. (Pick 21)

The argument presented above points at the complex referentiality that underlies the fabrication of both the metropolitan space and the penal colony. It might thus be rewarding to turn to Paul Gilroy's theory of the "Black Atlantic," which applies a reverse logic to common understandings of colonization by emphasizing that instead of giving birth to the new world, Europe gave birth to itself by a much needed referent—the colonies. Yet we have to extend this mirror image, because the penal colony was a prison setting on the colonial territory with people who had once been, or still were citizens of e.g. France. As Europe tried to define its metropolitan identity at the turn of the century (cf. Stoler and Cooper 1-30) it excluded parts of its population into the far-off regions which were then "occupied" by the racial discourse of colonialism. The "transportation," or "transplantation" into the zone required a phase of transition, which implied a spatial *exclusion*—the actual "journey" to the islands or colonies—and the *inclusion* into an already existing racial/social discourse of the Other.

Different groups then entered the realm of invisibility. Vagabonds, prostitutes, the insane, the poor peasantry or political opponents such as the June insurgents, were at times ascribed almost amorphous, animalistic and infantile qualities and were treated under the same law of subordination. As a "property of reason" they had to be taken care of and could neither speak nor act on their own behalf. In his groundbreaking study *Orientalism*, Edward Said has pointed out that these discourses of inferiority and degeneracy were projections originally forced upon the non-European world. Yet, he addresses, however limited, the interconnection of the Oriental and the Other within, "having in common an identity best described as *lamentably alien*" (my emphasis, Said 207). Similiarly Jean Borreil has emphasized that the word *prolétaire* etymologically refers to the one without-name, who, although he participated in social life, was symbolically and politically marginalized (24). In a more recent study on the penal colony in New Caledonia, Alice Bullard has further illuminated the intricate dynamics of the discourses of civilization and savagery, stressing that "[t]he lower classes, then, without speech, without ancestry, and without participation in humanity—the pursuit of which […] was identified by Guizot as civilization—seemed condemned to utter disenfranchisement" (18). As the Other became more visible in the city due to overpopulation caused by a rural exodus in the nineteenth century,[7] the anthropological "making of the object" (Fabian) did not only pertain to the legitimation of European domination over native cultures in the colonies, but also to the social classes within.

The island in this context provided a place of disposal, but more so, it became an analogous structure to the degenerated, peripheral status of the Other. The "penal island" on the colonized territory "housed" different social, cultural and political groups, which promised to be manageable problems within the "boundedness" and "remoteness" of the island. This was further facilitated by the emerging scientific discourses which treated certain social groups as „objects," or "species," and the island as "site," or "laboratory". The penal colony then provided "in essence a geographic technique, deploying instruments of distance and density" (Redfield 64).

---

7 In nineteenth-century France the numbers of people living in the urban areas almost tripled, the demographic changes, the rural exodus and the insufficient sanitary facilities and maintenance aggravated the conditions and prospects of the poor (Gillis 1989: 314).

The Island as Other

Islands have always played a crucial role in the economic and scientific development, but also in the cultural imaginary of the Western world. As a "master metaphor" (Gillis 3) they served a variety of meanings and projections, which have changed over time. In eighteenth and nineteenth scientific culture islands were portrayed as laboratory environments, which offered many "discursive possibilities" (Edmond and Smith 3) for an exploration of natural conditions or social configurations. In fact, "[t]he desire to perceive the island as a bounded and therefore controllable space seems to link writings on islands across the sciences and humanities, connecting the most fantastic of island utopias with the most careful of scientific treatises" (Edmond and Smith 5). Darwin's voyage to the Galapagos Islands, Wallace exploration of the Malay Archipelago and also the fictional travels to Moreau's island were equally developmental determinist narratives which presented the island as an enclosed space of experimentation (ibid.). For French Guiana, this idea has become reality with the establishment of the Ariane space program at Kourou. Peter Redfield poignantly describes how "[t]he technical spaces and natural places at the edge of things provide testing grounds, room for mistakes, leftovers, and visions of the past and future" (Redfield 26). Furthermore the idea of the island as a space of encounter also pertains to social and aesthetic experiments. The protagonist of *Papillon* traverses the different sceneries of the Other: the leper colony, the penal colony and the Native village. This simultaneity of the nonsimultaneous, was furthermore described in the memoir of René Belbenoit, a former convict of French Guiana, who depicted Devil's Island as a place of racial degeneration chosen to perform the "black, the yellow and the white experiment" (qtd. in Redfield 97).

The discourse of determinism and the trajectory of developmental narratives in the nineteenth century furthermore adapted a perception of islands that displayed a locus of utopian and sexual phantasies, of adventure and horror, (self)exploration and (self-)loss in the Western world. Within the evocations of a concentric world view, islands were subordinate to continental culture (Gillis 1-5), although at any time other narratives existed and "[i]t is unlikely that Pacific Islanders (…) shared the continental distinction between land and sea, and the colonial history of the Carribean is inscribed in ocean trajectories as well as island locations" (Edmond and Smith 2). Yet, in readings of the binary opposition of island and mainland, the islands offered a range of qualities which have fostered the island imaginary: boundedness, virginity, property, remoteness, *altérité*, perishability, and referentiality (cf. Gillis, Edmond and Smith; MacArthur and Wilson; Hamilton-Paterson; Beer; and Dening). For the metropolitan penal discourse attributes of "remoteness," "virginity" and "property" determined the discussion of a suitable locale. This is further indicated by the fact that the islands were perceived to be "natural colonies" (Edmond and Smith 3) and the colonies appeared to be "insular spaces."

Hence the idea of the penal colony as a colony and a penal island merged into a semantic field that dominated much of the nineteenth century statements of overseas penal colonies: In 1816, M. Forestier, a French bureaucrat issued a report entitled "Memoire sur le choix d'un lieu de deportation" in which he was eager to find objective criteria for the choice of suitable penal sites overseas. His treatise shows in how far the conceptions of the island affected the discussions of place in the debates of the penal colonies. Forestier comes to the conclusion that "a successful colony then should not have been too close, but also not too far, and represent a distinct settlement of its own (...)" offering a *"removal considerable enough to create an obstacle*, not only to their return, but also to communications with them, of which facility and frequency would not be without danger. *A place circumscribed, isolated, distanced from civil establishments*, be they national or foreign, where the deported might find ways of escape or the opportunity to create turmoil" (qtd. in Redfield 59). The sense of *property* also influenced ideas to implement certain model formations, as the structure of the English penal colonies was thought to be "transplantable"—New Caledonia then could surely become a "Sydney of France in Oceania" (Brainne qtd. in Forster, 150). As an anthropological place the island was "enacted" as a site of representation and as a representative place, where the penal and colonial/imperial discourses overlapped, contradicted and complemented each other. Literature and film illustrate and generate the production of the locale by referring to cultural legends and myth which anon serve as pretext's to constitute and explore the place of the island. One might ask how subversive these representations are, or in how far they are displaying a hierarchy that mirrors the social conceptions of continental Europe. Hence the "being" of islands is much more complex and aligned to *perceptions* and *desire,* not only in literature and the arts, but also within the scientific and social context of the colonial and imperial project. Keeping that in mind, a juxtaposition of imaginary and "real" accounts of the penal islands seems rather difficult to pursue.

Exploring the Island: Frank Schaffner's *Papillon* and Kafkas' "In the Penal Colony"

For some it might be questionable to turn to the Hollywood adaption of Henri Charriere's novel *Papillon* (1970). Critics, such as Alexander Miles and Steven Toth, have presented the film as the antipode to a historically "correct" image of the penal colony in French Guiana and New Caledonia. The "Introduction" of Toth's study then sets the tone:

> Even today, long after its theatrical premiere in 1973, images of a defiant and determined Steve McQueen running through the jungle and evading his cruel captors linger in the collective unconscious. Indeed, with the advent of VHS, cable televi-

sion, and worldwide film distribution, it is likely that *Charrière's story has never really stopped playing since its original release more than three decades ago.* As a result, two generations of viewers have learned of the penal colonies only through the distorted lens of a self-aggrandizing autobiography and Hollywood movie magic. *Therefore the bagnes [...] are distant and exotic, ensnared in myth and legend.* (my emphasis, Toth, xi)

Here the author provides me with at least two arguments to venture an analysis of the film. First of all, it seems almost negligent not to consider the cultural source of the collective and popular knowledge of the penal colonies. Toth himself implies that societies today, more than hundred years ago, define themselves via globalized televised images of the self and Other. Then how, one might ask, can a critical analysis concerning the images distributed, which have apparently become of almost universal value, ignore *Papillon*? What is the make-up of this "distorted image" (Toth xi) and can it be easily dismissed as elusive?[8] An interpretation of the film might provide us with a better understanding of the cultural myth and legends, which provide the master narratives of a still valid perception of the deviant/defiant.[9]

Whereas the film *Papillon* is probably the most well-known popular representation of the penal colony, the second narrative subject to analysis is the most cited canonical text in Western literature on the space of the penal colony: Franz Kafka's "In the Penal Colony". I depart from the assumption that both, film and short story, portray the island as a space of experience, but not as a space of life. The island is rather a way station, a liminal space—a place of metamorphosis, transformation and self-discovery for the European metropolitan subject. Moreover film and short story explore the insular existence as precarious and intricately interwoven with continental perceptions and in addition pertain to the argument that the space of the island is foremost constituted by movement, transition and the interaction of persons.

Already at the beginning of the film we are introduced to the *univers pénitencier*—a fractal structure, which by no means refers solely to the prison island or the penal colony, but here prefigures in a Metropolitan prison. The first minute shows the commandant of the institution, who, after having received a list of all convicts accounted for on the parade place, informs the crowd in front of him about the following procedure:

---

8   Pierre Dufour has argued that the Marquis de Sade has probably "opened" the prisons for literature. In fact, the world of literature in the eighteenth and nineteenth century was populated with convicts, and malfeasants in prisons and dungeons from Alexandre Dumas' *Comte de Monte Christo*, to Charles Dickinson's *Little Dorrit*, Victor Hugo's *Les Misérables*, or Zola's *Le Ventre de Paris* (358).

9   Between 1925 and 1955 a number of Hollywood films worked with the image of the French bagne: William Clemens' *Devil's Island* (1939) with Boris Karloff, *Le Cargo maudit* (1940) by Frank Borzage, with Clark Gable, Joan Crawford, Peter Lorre, or Michael Curtiz' *Passage to Marseille* with Humphrey Bogart (Dufour 326).

As for this moment you are the property of the penal administration, French Guiana. After serving your full terms in prison those of you with sentences of eight years or more will remain in Guiana as workers and colonists, for a period equal to that of your original sentences. As for France, the nation has disposed of you. France has rid herself of you altogether. (00:00:39-00:01:14)

With a shift of perspective from a close-up on the commandant, who further instructs the prisoners to "[f]orget France, and put your clothes on" (00:01:15-00:01:19), to a long-shot on the naked prisoners and the prison buildings in the background, the camera captures the hierarchies and the modes of surveillance employed. The panorama view instills all elements and perspectives essential to the space of control: the parade place, the walls, the barbwire, the watch tower with the armed guard, the other guards in uniform watching the prisoners standing in line, the commandant on a tribune addressing the prisoners, and the prison buildings. Hence the filmic perspective not only frames the carceral space, but is constitutive of its inner mechanism: the panopticon. The single parts, the figures, the arrangement and perspective fabricate the space of detention.

Here the metropolitan prison is the gateway for a further processing by the penal system, which also implies a further degradation of the prisoner's status within the community. The situation presented marks their entry into another state of existence as convicts, which bereaves them of a citizenship that is bound to the space of the metropolis and further defined by points of exit and entry. The walk through the city to board the galley then affirms their lower status which is focused from the high-angle perspective of the balconies: The city crowd watches the crowd of the convicts as they are taken down the streets to the harbor (00:01:28-00:02:38). The form of spectacle which was abolished with the enclosed space of the prison, is here revived in an image of public execution. In this respect Foucault might be right when he thinks of the penal colony as a more archaic form of punishment since the process of transition is similar to being sent to the block.

The story that follows revolves around two convicts who become friends while they try to survive the hardships of prison life in French Guiana. Luis Degas, a famous French counterfeiter sentenced to convict labor is in danger of being killed by the other convicts who know that he has enough money to bribe the guards and flee the islands. Papillon, who apparently has been framed and innocently sentenced for murder offers to protect him in exchange for the money he needs to escape.[10] Both men have to endure hard penal labor in the swamps, where they hunt down crocodiles and butterflies for tradesmen who are in cahoots with the guards. These merchants exploit the natural resources of French Guiana for their clients in North America who use the color of the blue

---

10 In another dream-sequence Papillon is accused by a judge for the even more serious offense of "having wasted his life" (00:55:19-00:55:27).

morpho butterfly as dye in the manufacture of American currency (00:35:34-00:35:38). After two unsuccessful attempts to escape the island, Papillon is condemned for lifetime to Devil's Island from where he can finally escape on a bag of coconuts while Degas stays behind.

Although the film right from the beginning is eager to depict the cruelty of the penal system, the convict life remains ambivalent and shifts between moments of recklessness and solidarity. Whereas the first scenes still victimize the convicts, the film gradually turns into a narrative of adventure in which the island offers possibilities of individualization and empowerment, primarily for the white male metropolitan subject. At the arrival at French Guiana, Papillon, Degas and some of the other prisoners stand on deck of the ship eying the Îles du Salut. Inherent to this posture is the double logic of the penal politics to equally abandon the ill elements of society and to colonize the land. In the scene they take up the position of the conquerors who measure points of entry and exit, of possibilities to master the island. The prisoners are still granted the right to represent by virtue of their origin. On deck of the galley a hierarchy is displayed which shall become one of the essential premises for Papillon's escape.

I assume that the film stages different forms and figurations of exclusion, from the imported slave, the Native, the leper and the convict which not only encapsulates a historical reality of many islands and territories of the South Pacific and the Atlantic, as Moloka'i, certain areas of French Guiana, or Robben Island have been slave plantations, leprosariums and penal colonies (cf. Edmond), but moreover defines the island as a kind of permanent spatial figuration of deviance.[11] However the possibilities of solidarity among the socially excluded are limited and portrayed as one-sided, as the "encounter" with the Other serves solely as a catalyst for Papillon's urge to return home.

In the following I will describe how these "contacts" configure *Papillon* as an adaption of the Odyssean adventure at whose core one finds the foundational narrative of a Western self-conception. There the island provides the structure of self-recognition via mechanism of exclusion and incorporation. Roger Moss has argued that "[f]rom the Odyssey onwards, islands have […] been represented as small, faraway and wild places, places of seductive enchantment or of monstrous threat that may be 'exotic' but are, by the same token, places to be escaped to, or escaped from, in a journey whose goal is 'home'" (146). Papillon, who equally perambulates the island, is confronted with deathly and miraculous encounters until he can finally escape "God's prison" (Redfield 104). As the prisoners arrive at French Guiana the area around the harbor of Kourou is portrayed as a resort for the socially dispensa-

---

11   In this regard the penal colony is an "abject zone", much like the squatter camp, the mental asylum, or the red-light district, as described by Anne MacClintock in her well-known study *Imperial Leather*.

ble: the traders (ex-convicts turned into man-hunters), prostitutes and ex-slaves await them. Their presence somehow foreshadows the fortune of those who have just arrived at French Guiana. The depiction of Kourou, which was the port of departure to the Îles du Salut, is characterized by violence and excess. The two most enthralling images of this arrival display the women of the brothel and a black woman, who is cutting the throat of a fish while the pigs and men are lying around in the mud. This environment anticipates further encounters with the Other and the morbidity of the penal colony.

At his second attempt to escape, Papillon comes to a leper colony where he wants to bribe his rifles for a boat. He is invited to enter a small hut which discloses a half-lit room with a group of people sitting around a table. For a moment one of the lepers leans into the light to make himself visible, yet the viewer's judgment is bound to Papillon's reaction who averts his gaze (01:36:09 –01:36:32). Offended by his behavior, the leper confronts him: "Why don't you have the courtesy to look at me when you speak?" (01:36:50). Papillon, who does not want to run the risk of displeasing the leper since he still needs the boat, accepts a further testing when the leper asks him to take a puff of his pipe. Only later will he be told that the leper of the man across from him is not contagious. Alluding to the Odyssee, Papillon equally faces dangerous and deathly threats. Yet, the successful "traversal" of the island contains a form of incorporation and integration of the Other into the own narrative which exhibits his own exceptionality. Papillon measures his free will at the boundedness of the Other, meaning either their corporeal disabilities (the leper) or their inability to adapt to Western civilization (the Native). This structure of self-discovery and empowerment has been further illuminated by Adorno and Horkheimer in the *Dialectics of Enlightenment*:

> All the adventures Odysseus survives are dangerous temptations deflecting the self from the path of its logic. [..] [T]he knowledge which makes up his identity and enables him to survive has its substance in the experience of diversity, distraction, disintegration; the knowing survivor is also the man who exposes himself most daringly to the threat of death, thus gaining the hardness and strength to live. (38)

The leper colony, as a community of the living death, could be paralleled to the island of the Cyclopes, the barbaric cannibals who kill everyone who trespasses their territory. The indigenous village, where Papillon takes shelter at his second escape, however, displays similarities to the island of Circe. The dream-like sequence which shows Papillon in the village of the Amerindos takes on the form of forgetting, a state of pre-historical comfort. As Adorno and Horkheimer further imply, "magic"—Circes instrument—"disintegrates the self which falls back into its power and thus into a form of an earlier biological species" (38). The indigenous girl who takes care of Papillon furthermore alludes to the hetaira and displays a romantic image of the noble savage. Yet, similar to Odysseus, Papillon needs to wake from his dream to continue his journey home. After he has tattooed the motif of the Papillon on the chest of the clan chief he falls asleep and shortly after finds the village abandoned. Here the film addresses the annexation of the land by the colonizer, the inscription of Western culture and the consequent disappearance of the indigenous culture. Nevertheless, the chimerical image of the Native contains a problematic notion of the indigenous people as they move into the mythical realm and constitute a dream from which modern man necessarily has to wake in order to reach his goal—the metropolis, meaning civilization. With the awakening and the breaking of the spell, the indigenous people have to vanish, since they have fulfilled their duty—their time, so to say, is up.

So even though the "contact" is characterized by gestures of solidarity and a glimpse of mutual respect, Papillon's escape exposes a hierarchy between different forms of the socially excluded. Throughout the film Papillon is in danger of being affected or infected by the *altérité*—the deathly Other of the island as represented by the leper, the Amerindo-girl and the disciplining penal administration. Especially the first two groups seem to be generically bound to the island in their characteristics of immobility, excess (sexually) and violence. In the end Papillon is a hybrid figure between the physically superior Hercules and the sly Odysseus who survives the two modes of decay: the physical (biological) in the figure of the leper, and the mental (cultural) decay in the figure of the indigenous. The ill and the "savage" are left behind at the island—and yet another group—the "common" convict.

Towards the end of the film and shortly before he can finally escape the penal colony, Papillon takes a rest on a stone bench atop a cliff on Devil's Island. A convict passes by and yells at him for defiling the bench of Captain Dreyfus who used to sit there. He asks him who he thinks he is and Papillon responds "Nobody", just as Odysseus replied to the Cyclope Polyphemus (02:06:23-02:06:46). As "Odysseus, the subject, denies his own identity, which makes him a subject, and preserves his life by mimicking the amorphous realm" (Adorno and Horkheimer 53), Papillon makes himself disappear and thus distinguishes himself from the other prisoner, who is, within this reading, "not a self" (ibid.). In the end Papillon survives because he refuses and successfully averts the affiliation with any form of collectivity and thus makes his individualism his strength (Horkheimer 53-54).

Similarly Kafka's parable depicts the insular penal colony as a space of experience of/for a modern metropolitan culture and not so much as a space of the "proper" life. Yet, how does this assumption figure in the personae and the perspective of Kafka's "In the Penal Colony"? First I would argue in the representation of the "explorer" as a man of science, and second in the strategies of seduction employed to draw the explorer into the realm of the archaic procedures of torture and violence as presented by the "officer". Through perspective and figuration both film and text weave the metropolitan discourse of civilization and the discourse of savagery into a complex space.

The story of takes place at a colony somewhere "in the tropics" to which a French speaking explorer has traveled to investigate the local penal practices. He is attended to by an officer who formerly belonged to the staff of the old regime and now pursues the execution at place. A convict who has been charged for disobedience is signed up for execution at the explorer's arrival, which equally presents the perfect opportunity for the officer to promote an apparatus that had been designed by the Old Commandant for the sole purpose of punishment. While the officer explains the working of the "remarkable piece of apparatus" (Kafka 89), he concomitantly tries to convince his guest to support him in front of the New Commandant, who plans to abolish the inhumane practice. As the explorer continues to refuse any involvement, the officer accepts his fate, frees the convict and lies down on the "bed" of the apparatus himself. He is killed by the machine which destroys itself during the procedure. After having witnessed the officer's death, the explorer visits the grave of the Old Commandant and then hastily leaves the island. On the dockyard he threatens the convict and a soldier, who had been called to the execution, with a knotted rope as they try to jump on the boat that takes him away.

My analysis intersects with the socio-cultural perspectives and findings of Walter Müller-Seidel, Paul Peters, Peter Neumeyer and John Zilcosky, who have pointed out that "The Penal Colony" not only relates to a historical reality of the penal islands, but also to a rich intertextual archive from pulp chronicles such as Schaffenstein's *Little Green Books* (*Grüne Bändchen*) (cf. Neumeyer), to the reports of German colonial civil servants from the Pacific region, e.g. Robert Heindl's "Eine Forschungsreise nach den Strafkolonien" (1912)—a description of the conditions of the penal systems in New Caledonia, Australia, and China. Kafka was also familiar with the writings of Charles Darwin's *Theory of Evolution* and had followed the public debate on the importance of penal colonies which was influenced by one of his teachers, Hans Groß, whose book *Degeneration and Deportation* (1905/06) combined evolutionary, determinist and judicial discourses of the time (cf. Müller-Seidel). Furthermore "In the Penal Colony" reflects readings of novels and semi-fictional narratives like Octave Mirbeau's *Jardin des supplices* and Fyodor Dostojevsky's *Notes from the Death House*, which, much like the colonial reports, presented protagonists from the city, as doctors, engineers, writers, but also convicts and adventurers who were send to far off regions in order to either explore the local cultures, or to serve sentences.

Although I cannot dismiss the ongoing debate on whether there is "an actual historical topography" to Kafka's *Penal Colony*, I would agree with Paul Peters to assume that we find it in "the landscape of colonialism" (Peters 401). Kafka himself has mentioned in his diaries that the colonial adventure stories in the *Little Green Books* have been a *Vor-Schrift* for his own writing and life (cf. Neumeyer). One of Kafka's most favorite books of these volumes was Oscar Weber's *The Sugar Baron: The Adventures of a former German Officer in*

South America (Der Zuckerbaron: Schicksale eines ehemaligen deutschen Offiziers in Südamerika)—a story that presented "the fin de siècle practice of colonial sadism" (Zilcosky 106). John Zilcolsky understands the "rules" Kafka refers to as a "prescription," "a system of writing," which "captures the notion of pre-writing or pre-text" (106). He also proposes that Kafka "understood them [the books], in the Foucauldian sense, as part of a discourse of adventure and colonialism" (106-7). The Penal Colony then again presents the island as a space of experience, *and* as an experimental space of writing, allowing Kafka to conceive seemingly opposing systems and beliefs. He presents the penal colony as "a hybrid [...] part machine, part beast" (Redfield 64), connecting Weberian bureaucracy and an almost pre-modern system of torture and spectacle. Moreover, in the ambivalence of the characters, the perspective and the constitution of the place, the discursive space of the colony and the metropolis, of Old and New Imperialism, merge, and are revealed to work upon the same mechanism: violence, voyeurism and sadism. Kafka no longer presents the island as an antithetical space, but as a space constituted and constantly recovered by man, moreover the space itself becomes a fabric built into the matrix of modern thought through acts of seduction and desire.

In the story the officer wants to convert the explorer by making him aware of the extraordinary construction of the machine. He tries to convince him to touch and look at certain parts: "Wouldn't you care to come a little nearer and have a look at the needles?" (99). Yet at first place his enthusiastic promotion of the apparatus, which clearly draws on sexual connotations, are ineffective since the explorer turns away and refuses to take up his part as spectator. Although at some point the explorer admires the Old Commandant for his multiple talents to design and build the machine, in the end the officer can only win over the explorer by sacrificing himself. He forces the explorer into the role of the audience, which then revivifies the culture of spectacle carried out under the Old Commandant. This economy of seduction is crucial for the understanding of the story, since the explorer's attitude, as critics such as Peters, or Zilcosky have argued, is closely linked to the reform movement of the last decade of the nineteenth century, which had criticized the "unapologetic Old Imperialism" (Zilcosky 110) for their "fantasies of domination, violence and pleasure" (ibid.). Yet the hypocracy of the reformists becomes evident in the figure of the explorer at the moment he turns into the accomplice of the system. His objective mission to solely "observe" is tainted in the moment he partakes in the execution of the officer as his distinguished guest and further discredited at the end of the story when the explorer threatens the soldier and the convict with a knotted rope in order to prevent them from jumping on board.

Eventually the well-being and the position of the explorer depend on the system of colonialism, the island necessarily has to remain a way station—a laboratory to secure the existence of an arsenal of figures of "missionaries, educators, and doctors [who] could carry out experiments in social engineering without confronting the popular resistances and bourgeois rigidities of European society at home" (Stoler and Cooper 5). This also means that the explorer necessarily needs to leave them behind to secure his own existence within the exploitive structures of an "enlightened" system. Here Kafka's penal colony exposes a "politics of distinction" on different levels. First the explorer tries to distance himself from the penal practice on site, yet in the course of the narrative his behavior reveals his fundamental dependency on the despotic and sadistic colonial regime which is then the sphere of his exceptionalism. His position also seems to imply a rejection of the condemned man, the soldier and the "poor" dockyard laborers (Kafka 126). The explorer seems far from having pity or sympathy particularly for the convict, since he describes him as "a stupid-looking wide-mouthed creature with bewildered hair and face," reminding the explorer of "a submissive dog that one might have thought he could be left to run free on the surrounding hills and would only need to be whistled for when the execution was due to begin" (Kafka 89).

Although *Papillon* exhibits similar forms of encounter and attempts of seduction, the protagonist can successfully avert the threat of being drawn into the world of the Other, he "passes" the lepers, the indigenous culture and the French penal administration and gains a moral strength for which he is finally rewarded. Kafka's explorer, on the contrary, has discovered or rather, recovered, his own *altérité*, the savage Other within himself, a sadistic and violent inheritance that he as a man of the *theoría* had wanted to circumvent by trying not to get involved in the politics of the penal colony:

> The explorer thought to himself: It's always a ticklish matter to intervene decisively in other people's affairs. He was neither a member of the penal colony nor a citizen of the state to which it belonged. Were he to denounce this execution or actually try to stop it, they could say to him: You are a foreigner, mind your own business. He could make no answer to that, unless he were to add that he was amazed at himself in this connection, for he traveled only as an observer, with no intention at all of altering other people's methods of administering justice. Yet here he found himself strongly tempted. The injustice of the procedure and the inhumanity of the execution were undeniable. No one could suppose that he had any selfish interest in the matter, for the condemned man was a complete stranger, not a fellow countryman or even at all sympathetic to him. (Kafka 105)

Indeed, the explorer traveled only "to observe" (Kafka 105) yet the "coquetry between officer and voyager" (Zilcosky 113) exposes the scientific lens as veiled, even more, as being constituted by voyeuristic drives. In the end both figures, explorer and officer, are bound together in the prophecy of the Old Commandant which promises the return of the old regime: "Here rests the old Commandant. His adherents, who now must be nameless, have dug this grave and set up this stone. There is a prophecy that after a certain number of years the Commandant will rise again and lead his adherents from this house to recover the colony. Have faith and wait!" (126). The inscription has become part of the topography of the island, the grave of the Old Commandant is set up in the teahouse, which equally binds the system of trade with the despotic realm. The grave of the Old commandant ultimately alludes to the chthonic remains of power. Here again, the idea of revolution is built into the very landscape of the colony as nineteenth century racial theories proclaimed, yet it is not the "indigenous savage" that threatens to rise, but the "civilized savage" in the sadistic system of colonization itself. Kafka's text then exposes a position of negation and denial at the heart of our enlightened societies for what is excluded and furthermore a certain politics of distinction that is based on desire.

However, the island as a space of desire and exclusion is by no means a phenomenon of the nineteenth and early twentieth century, but extends far into the present. As for our time it seems that another figure has been appropriated by the mechanisms of marginalization: the illegal immigrant. Rod Edmond has emphasized that the leper colonies Nauru or Magokai in Australia experience a revival as sites of exclusion under the conditions of global migration:

> If lepers were one of the main pariah groups of the colonial world at the turn of the twentieth century, refugees and asylum seekers, commonly dismissed as illegal immigrants, have an equivalent status at the beginning of the twenty-first. In both cases islands have been used as dumping grounds for the unwanted and as a defence system for mainlands that consider themselves beleaguered. (Edmond 143)

Yet as these "island solutions" proved to be ineffective in creating an obstacle, the Australian government went even one step further in its 2001 Migration Amendment Act by "excising hundreds of small islands off the north coast from the country's migration zone. This means that people who reach these islands can no longer claim refugee status. [...] In order to preserve the health and integrity of the nation its islands are being looped off and cast adrift" (Edmond 143). Since the numbers of those who enter the terrain of the islands become unmanageable, the islands themselves are cut off and disposed from the national territory in order to secure and protect the rights of its "proper" citizens. The islands still delineate a deathly space for a group of people whose presence poses a threat so dangerous that the government rather hazards the consequences of losing sovereignty over parts of its national holdings.

Works Cited

Arendt, Hannah. *The Origins of Totalitarianism*. New York: Harcourt, Brace & Co., 1951.

Borreil, Jean ed. "Présentation". *Les sauvages dans la cité: auto-émancipation du peuple et instruction des prolétaires au XIXe siècle*. Paris: Champ Vallon, 1985. 21-31.

Boucon, Honoret. *Les Parias de Guyane. Les Parias de la Guyane*, étude documentaire sur la transportation colonial. éditions de "l'Aide sociale, 1913.

Bullard, Alice. *Exile to Paradise. Savagery and civilization in Paris and the South Pacific, 1790-1900*. Stanford: Stanford Univ. Press, 2000.

Christopher, Emma. *"A Merciless Place". The Lost Story of Britain's Convict Disaster in Africa*. Oxford: Oxford Univ. Press, 2011.

Cooper, Frederick, and Stoler, Ann Laura ed. "Between Metropole and Colony. Rethinking a Research Agenda". *Tensions of Empire. Colonial Cultures in a Bourgeois World*. Berkeley: Univ. of California Press, 1997. 1-56.

Da Passano, Mario ed. *Europäische Strafkolonien im 19. Jahrhundert: internationaler Kongress des Dipartimento di Storia der Universität Sassari und der Parco Nazionale di Asinara, Porto Torres, 25. Mai 2001*. Berlin: BWV, Berliner Wiss.-Verl., 2006.

Dufour, Pierre. *Les bagnes de Guyane*. Paris: Pygmalion, 2006.

Edmond, Rod. "Abject bodies / Abject Sites: Leper Island in the High Imperial Era." *Islands in History and Representation*. Ed. Rod Edmond and Vanessa Smith. New York: Routledge, 2003. 133-145.

Edmond, Rod, and Smith, Vanessa. "Editor's Introduction". *Islands in History and Representation*. Ed. Rod Edmond and Vanessa Smith. New York: Routledge, 2003. 1-18.

Fabian, Johannes. *Time and the Other. How Anthropology Makes its Object*. New York: Columbia Univ. Press, 2002.

Forster, Colin. „French Penal Policy and the Origins of the French Presence in New Caledonia". *Journal of Pacific History*, 26 (1991): 135-150.

Foucault, Michel. *Discipline and Punish: The Birth of the Prison*. New York: Vintage Books, 1979 [1975].

---. Michel. *Power/Knowledge: Selected Interviews and Other Writings, 1972-1977*. Ed. Colin Gordon. New York: Pantheon, 1980.

Gillis, John R. *Islands of the Mind. How the Human Imagination Created the Atlantic World*. New York: Palgrave, 2004.

Gillis, A.R. "Crime and State Surveillance in Nineteenth Century France". *American Journal of Sociology*. Vol. 95, No. 2 (September 1989): 307-41.

Gilroy, Paul. *The Black Atlantic: Modernity and Double Consciousness*. 3. Impr., Reprint. London: Verso, 2002.

Horkheimer, Max, and Adorno, Theodor W. *Dialectic of Enlightenment*. Ed. Gunzelin Schmid Noerr. Trans. Edmund Jephcott. Stanford: Stanford Univ. Press, 2002.

Kafka, Franz. „In the Penal Colony". *Selected Short Stories of Franz Kafka*. Trans. Willa and Edwin Muir. New York: Random House, 1952.

Lowenthal, David. "Colonial Experiments in French Guiana, 1760-1800. *The Hispanic Historical Review*. Vol. 32, No. 1 (Feb., 1952): 22-43.

MacClintock, Anne. *Imperial Leather: Race, Gender and Sexuality in the Colonial Contest*. New York: Routledge, 1995.

McClintock, Scott. "The Penal Colony: Inscritption of the Subject in Literature, Law, and Detainees as Legal Non-Persons at Camp X-Ray. *Comparative Literature Studies*. Vol 41, No. 1 (2004): 153-167.

Miles, Alexander. *Devil's Island: Colony of the Damned*. Berkeley: Ten Speed Press, 1988.

Morgan, Gwenda, and Rushton, Peter. *Eighteenth-century Criminal Transportation: the Formation of the Criminal Atlantic*. Basingstroke: Palgrave MacMillan, 2004.

Moss, Roger. "Derek Walcott's Omeros: Representing St. Lucia, Re-presenting Homer". *Islands in History and Representation*. Ed. Rod Edmond and Vanessa Smith. New York: Routledge, 2003. 146-161.

Müller-Seidel, Walter. *Die Deportation des Menschen: Kafkas Erzählung "In der Strafkolonie" im europäischen Kontext*. München: Fischer, 1989.

Neumeyer, Peter. "Franz Kafka, Sugar Baron". *Modern Fiction Studies*. 17, No. 1 (Spring 1971): 5-16.

O'Brien, Patricia. *The Promise of Punishment: Prisons in Nineteenth-Century France*. Princeton: Princeton Univ. Press, 1982.

Papillon. 1973. Dir. Franklin J. Schaffner. Perf. Steve McQueen, Dustin Hoffmann. Sony Pictures Home Entertainment, 2000.

Pick, Daniel. *Faces of Degeneration: a European Disorder, 1848-1918*. Cambridge [u.a.]: Cambridge Univ. Pr., 1989.

Piper, Karen. "The Language of the Machine: A Postcolonial Reading of Kafka." *Journal of the Kafka Society of America*. Vol. 20, No. 1-2 (1996): 42-54.

Peters, Paul. "Witness to the Execution: Kafka and Colonialism." *Monatshefte* Vol. 93, No. 4 (2001): 401-125.

Petit, Jacques-Guy ed. *Histoire des galères, bagnes er prisons: XIIe – Xxe siècles. Introduction à l'histoire pénale de la France*. Toulouse: Privat, 1991.

Redfield, Peter. "Foucault in the Tropics. Displacing the Panopticon". *Anthropologies of Modernity. Foucault, Governmentality, and Life Politics*. Ed. Jonathan Xavier Inda. Malden: Blackwell Publishing Ltd, 2005. 50-79.

Redfield, Peter. *Space in the Tropics. From Convicts to Rockets in French Guiana*. Berkeley: Univ. of California Press, 2000.

Said, Edward. *Orientalism*. London/Henley: Routledge & Kegan Paul, 1978.

Smith, Caleb. *The Prison and the American Imagination*. New Haven: Yale Univ. Press, 2009.

Toth, Stephen. *Beyond Papillon: the French Overseas Penal Colonies, 1854-1952*. Lincoln: Univ. of Nebraska Press, 2006.

Zilcosky, John. *Kafka's Travels. Exoticism, Colonialism, and the Traffic of Writing*. New York: Palgrave, 2003.

Zysberg, André. "Le bagne". *Histoire des galères, bagnes et prisons: XIIIe – Xxe siècles. Introduction à l'histoire pénale de la France*. Ed. Jacques-Guy Petit. Toulouse: Privat, 1991. 169-259.

Notes on Contributors

Rüdiger Kunow, former President of the German Association for American Studies and Professor and Chair of American Studies, Potsdam University, has taught at the Universities of Wuerzburg, Nürnberg-Erlangen, Freiburg, Hanover, and Magdeburg. He was a Research Fellow at the University of California, Santa Cruz and the State University of New York at Albany. His areas of research include transnationalisms (diaspora, migration, identity politics), the cultural imagination of aging, AIDS narratives and the Indian diaspora in the US and Canada. He is editor, with Heike Hartung of the thematic issue on "Age Studies" of the journal Amerikastudien/American Studies (2011), with Renate Brosch, of *Transgressions: Cultural Interventions in the Global Manifold* (2005), and author of *Das Klischee: Reproduzierte Wirklichkeiten in der englischen und amerikanischen Literatur* (1994).

Antonia Mehnert is a Ph.D. candidate at the University of Munich (American Studies Department), working on her dissertation project entitled "The Cultural Imaginary of Climate Change". She is furthermore participating in the structured doctoral program "Environment and Society" at the Rachel Carson Center. For her dissertation project she receives a scholarship from the Foundation of German Business. Antonia Mehnert studied American Studies, Latin-American studies and Economics at the University of Potsdam and the Free University Berlin. Her research interests include ecocriticism, Chicano/a Studies, the Caribbean, transnationalism, postcolonialism.

Frederike Offizier is a Ph.D. student at the American Studies Department of the University of Potsdam. Her dissertation focuses on dynamics of risk narratives and affects in U.S.-American literature and culture. She finished her double major in American Studies and Spanish Philology in 2011 with the MA thesis "DeComposing the Self: Dying in American Literature", for which she received the Hans-Jürgen-Bachorski-Preis from the University of Potsdam. She is currently employed as a research assistant and lecturer at the American Studies department of the University of Potsdam teaching literary and cultural studies classes. Her main research interests are transnationalism, Latino/a culture, cultural theory, and bioculture.

Sandra Poppe is Junior Professor of Comparative Literature at the University of Mainz, Germany. Her research focuses on literature and film, literature and the other arts, visuality, death and mourning in contemporary arts. Previous publications include: *Visualität in Literatur und Film. Eine medienkomparatistische Untersuchung moderner Erzähltexte und ihrer Verfilmungen* (2007). She is also co-editor of *Emotionen in Literatur und Film* (2011), *9/11 als kulturelle*

Zäsur. Repräsentationen des 11. September 2001 in kulturellen Diskursen, Literatur und visuellen Medien (2009), and *Franz Kafka: The Collected Works* (2007/2008). She is currently working on a book on fear and anxiety in the literature of the 19th and 20th centuries.

Marc Priewe is currently a substitute Professor of North American Literature and Culture at the University of Duisburg-Essen, Germany. From 2007 to 2008 he worked as a Visiting Assistant Professor of Early American Literature at St. Lawrence University, USA. In 2009 he was a Fulbright Visiting Scholar at the History of American Civilization Program, Harvard University. His publications include *Writing Transit: Refiguring National Imaginaries in Chicana/o Narratives* (2007) and *Imagined Transnationalism: U.S-Latino/a Literature, Culture, and Identity* (co-edited, 2009). His second monograph deals with literary and cultural representations of illness, healing, and medicine in colonial New England and is funded by the Germany Research Foundation.

John Carlos Rowe is USC Associate's Professor of the Humanities at the University of Southern California. He is the author of nine books, the editor of nine other titles, and has published more than 150 essays and reviews. He has published widely on Henry James, the intersections of nineteenth-century American literature and postmodern theory and U.S. imperialism. His most recently published books are *Afterlives of Modernism: Liberalism, Transnationalism, and Political Critique* (2011) and *The Cultural Politics of the New American Studies* (2012).

Ariane Schröder is a lecture and research associate at the American Studies Department of the University of Potsdam. She received her MA degree in May 2009. For her master thesis "Write or Be Written Of(f)" she was awarded the Hans-Jürgen-Bachorski-Preis of the University of Potsdam for the best master thesis in the Humanities. She is currently working towards her Ph.D. and her dissertation focuses on the relationship between cultural constructions of contagious disease and U.S. American Gothic literature.

Stephanie Siewert is a Ph.D. candidate in Comparative Literature at the University of Potsdam and a fellow of the Studienstiftung des deutschen Volkes. She received her M.A. degree in American Studies, Comparative Literature and Educational Science with a thesis on melancholy in contemporary transnational literatures. Her dissertation project focuses on carceral spaces and modalities of social visibility in literature and film in the 19th and 20th centuries. She is the co-editor of the essay collection *Spaces of Desire—Spaces of Transition. Space and Emotion in Modern Literature* (2011). Her main research interests include theories of space, ethical criticism, critical theory, and cultures of/in mobility.